EXPERTS' ENDORSEMENTS:

"Gail Kauranen Jones teaches us, through her generous and soulful example, that a meaningful life, one lived with purpose and passion, is above all an inner ongoing journey, available to all."

—Cliff Hakim, career and executive coach,
author of *We Are All Self-Employed*

* * *

"Gail Kauranen Jones accurately describes in *To Hell and Back... Healing Your Way Through Transition* the deeply psychological and spiritual process of change. As a result, she teaches the reader that it is the gradual internal shifts—not external circumstances—that lead to greater peace of mind and fulfillment."

—Dijana Winter, M. Ed., psychotherapist and life
coach with practices in Newburyport, MA and
Rochester, NY

TO HELL AND BACK...

HEALING YOUR WAY THROUGH TRANSITION

GAIL KAURANEN JONES

HATS
OFF

To Hell and Back...Healing Your Way through Transition

Published by Hats Off Books®
610 East Delano Street, Suite 104, Tucson, Arizona 85705 U.S.A.
www.hatsoffbooks.com

International Standard Book Number: 1-58736-269-4
Library of Congress Control Number: 2003097292

To Catie and Brendan, my gifts from God:

I thank you for all the joy and goodness you've brought to my life.

Table of Contents

ACKNOWLEDGMENTS

Writing a book about transition, especially one's own, is an evolving process. I am not the same person I was when I began my inner journeys detailed within. Fortunately, many of the people who have been part of my life during the twelve-year period of completing this book are still an integral part of my joy and well-being. I feel blessed by the richness they brought to my life. Some people I've parted ways with, through death, distance, disagreement, or self-respect. I am still indebted to these others for the life lessons they taught me.

To my family—Catie and Brendan Jones, and Wayne Kauranen—I am most grateful for your presence in my life. My children, Catie and Brendan, you allow me every day to know God exists as I watch the miracle of your lives unfold. I applaud my brother, Wayne, for taking over the lead role in my mother's caretaking issues, and for being such a good father to his children. And Skip Jones, the father of my children, I thank you for your technical expertise early on in this project.

To the most loyal of friends—Gail McMeekin, Darlene Adams, Marj Elliott, Wendy Higgins, Bess Zarafonitis Stroh, and Ellen Lawlor—your support carried me during my most terrifying moments of change. Each of you held me in highest regard, even when I didn't think I deserved your accolades. Darlene, your generosity also enabled me to market more professionally two of my businesses. Gail, your success as a writer inspired me to express myself similarly. Susan Harper and Nancy Prebble Barrett added many moments of fun to mothering young children.

To those who helped me heal deep wounds and taught me new life skills—Andrea Szymt, Dijana Winter, Flo Gaia, Brian Connelly,

Joy Davey, and Lawrence Stibbards—I thank you for bearing witness to my transformation and guiding me through the rough spots. Everyone needs a third-party observer now and then. Rather than be feared as some sort of failure on our part, receiving counseling is a gift we give ourselves, which hopefully benefits those around us. I am a better friend, mother, partner, teacher, and life coach because I took the time to unearth my past.

Cliff Hakim, Jennifer Niskala, Patricia Pegg, Linda Salazar, Lee Young, and Summer Mullins—you so generously gave me your writing and editing expertise. Each of you in your unique ways raised my standards of excellence and the quality of my life.

Lisa Franklin, my personal trainer and neighbor, you believed in this book and me. I am most grateful, however, for your physical and emotional presence during two scary years when I felt like I was losing everything in the world I ever loved. Your private fitness studio was both a safety net and a sanctuary.

Another contributor to this book's evolution is René Fabbri, the contractor who built my home studio, where I completed in peace the final manuscript. René, you honored my vision for "a room of her own" and made it even better. Lisa Kawski, you helped refine the space.

My workshop participants and coaching clients added much value to my life, too, grounding me in the joy of doing work I love, even when the world around me felt chaotic.

Cynde Bierman has been my very own Mary Poppins, loving my children almost as much as I do, and teaching them all the fun activities I never learned as a child. Cynde, you've brought the most enduring and irreplaceable gifts to our lives: the added joy and laughter that resonates within our home. Christine Whelton and Allison MacEachern, you both also gave much love to my children and provided more sanity to my life.

And lastly, but certainly not least, I thank Wilbur Doctor, the former chairman of the journalism department at the University of Rhode Island. I believe many defining moments in life occur when someone sees us in a higher, greater capacity than we see ourselves. Wilbur plucked me out from the crowd of sophomore journalism students and encouraged me as a writer. He was my first and toughest mentor and a very fine and respected human being.

PREFACE

In searching for the right title for this book, I kept hearing people tell me that they've been "to hell and back." My hairdresser—a recovering alcoholic—used the phrase to describe his journey to health. A friend, whose father died in a car accident, said her grief was like a trip into hell. Another acquaintance, going through a divorce, described his crazy yet perfectly normal feelings of disorientation as "hellish."

Each of these people's stories involved a transition, a moving from one way of being in the world to another—drunk to sober, loving daughter to fatherless woman, married to single.

The pain or "hell" each experienced led them into a new life, yet the inner reorganizing of their psyches that propelled them forward or "back" was done privately.

Many of us don't share our stories of growth until we've reached the other side of transition, where we feel whole and centered again. The ripe in-between time of healing is kept a secret, leaving many of us clueless about how to integrate change.

In *To Hell and Back...Healing Your Way through Transition*, I offer you intimate glimpses into four of my adult passages, hoping as a teacher and personal and business coach to guide you through the vulnerable moments that lead to new life.

The truth is that in transition we don't simply move forward. We first need to grieve the past and endure some time, not knowing what's next, before we move on to a new beginning. The time stuck not knowing which direction we are moving toward is the most difficult challenge for most of us.

"The problem is not that we don't want to give up a job or relationship, or that we can't let go our identity or our reality; the problem is that before we find a new something, we must deal with a time of nothing," according to William Bridges, author of *Transitions*.

Spending time doing nothing runs contrary to our consumer-driven, materialistic culture that teaches us to pursue change through external activity. Buy more, hopefully bigger and better items. Splurge on the luxury vacation that you may have to work longer hours to obtain, and when you finally take the time off, be sure you bring your cell phone and laptop computer along. Sign your kids up for as many activities as possible, so they, too, can stay so busy they don't have to learn to think for themselves, like how to be creative with downtime.

To Hell and Back...Healing Your Way through Transition teaches that real, lasting change is an internal process, not an external action. There is no quick fix. This "process" can take between one and three years, according to Ross Goldstein, author of *fortysomething*. I say life is a transition, with each day giving us new opportunities to redefine ourselves.

I think of transition as an unfolding of our souls. Each transition in our life—whether we change careers, become a mother, parent a parent, or bury a loved one—is an opportunity for personal growth. Some transitions are frightening wake-up calls, while others are gentle reminders that we're heading in the right direction. All can bring us closer to our authentic selves.

From my own experience and from teaching others the transition process, I know this for sure: Nothing you acquire will give you the same level of joy as a fully expressed soul.

I also believe each transition led me closer to healing within myself some very deep wounds. These transitions, which became stopping points to reevaluate my life's circumstances, were uncomfortable. Up until I changed careers, which was the first transition I embraced of which I was fully aware, I had lived my life on a treadmill, moving as fast as I could to get ahead. What I really got ahead of was myself.

That transition, and the subsequent ones I experienced, gave me a chance to catch up with my soul, which was lost for a very long time in frantic activity.

As a woman, I used my transitions to forge a new path for myself—one that enabled me to blend my life commitments. I realized that although I've long admired strong, inspiring women like

Oprah, life coach Cheryl Richardson, and *New York Times* best-selling author Nuala O'Faolain, I could not emulate them.

I wanted to create a life that enabled me to mother my children well, while fulfilling other creative urges. These women—two unmarried, all three without children—could no longer be my role models. In fact, I discovered that I didn't have any mother mentors. I knew I had to go within to find my answers.

To Hell and Back...Healing Your Way through Transition is my search for authenticity. Within that search, I offer you the guidance I gleaned from more than twelve years of research on the process of change.

Your journey will be different from mine because you are unique. In your discoveries, you will bring forth your own insights, talents, and purpose for living. May this book serve as a both a teacher and supportive friend, encouraging you to move beyond the rough spots to find a secure inner place of being that no external circumstance can ever threaten.

I. CHANGING CAREERS

Introduction

The dynamic tension between the known and unknown is more or less constant during adult life, though the balance is usually weighted on one side or the other ... Times when the urge to change becomes dominant are called transitions.

—Ross Goldstein, *fortysomething*

The average American can expect to change careers between four and six times over his or her lifetime, according to the National Bureau of Labor Statistics. The same bureau reports that in February 2000, the median number of years salaried workers had been with their current employer was 3.5 years.

Every day at least eighty thousand people consider a career change, and up to fifty million challenge the notion of a single career over a lifetime, according to Carole Hyatt, author of *Shifting Gears*. In her other book, *When Smart People Fail*, Hyatt maintains, "The average American will work for 10 different employers, keep each job only 3.6 years, and change his entire career three times before retirement." According to Ross Goldstein, author of *fortysomething*, "Multiple careers are the norm now."

The Internet website CareerJournal.com reports that individuals will have between three and five careers and hold seven to fifteen specific jobs over a lifetime.

The days of long-term job security ended with the recession of the early 1990s when the nation shifted from a manufacturing-based to a service-based economy. The most recent recession of 2003 confirmed what author and career and executive coach Cliff Hakim has been teaching for years: We are all self-employed.

World events—including the terrorist attacks, the war with Iraq, and the Enron-like corporate scandals—altered many people's priorities, with some adults now questioning for the first time the purpose of their lives.

Yet career change is not just about searching for meaning. Many people leave careers in pursuit of more money, greater professional challenges, and increased opportunities for self-expression.

Despite the frequency of anticipated change, there is relatively little information available about the emotional process of switching careers. Numerous books address finding a job, exiting the fast track, or pursuing a dream; they hint about life before and after switching careers, but they don't focus on the change itself.

I suspect there are several reasons for the lack of guidance on changing careers.

First of all, many people don't successfully change careers. They sabotage their transition by:

- rushing ahead to a different but unsuitable job;
- settling for the status quo;
- getting seduced back to the job they left for fear of trying something new;
- not making time for the "heavy lifting," figuring out what they really care about; and
- denying change is necessary.

Second, and perhaps most important, it is not commonly understood that a career transition is more of an inward journey than an external action. *It's a process of self-discovery, not just a job hunt.*

Work can be an expression of our inner selves, providing us with joy and power when it reflects honestly and accurately who we are. We find dissatisfaction in work when we use it to defend ourselves from our insecurities and shortcomings, repressing our needs in the process. As Barbara Sher so wittingly points out in her book *Wishcraft*, "Contrary to what you may have been taught, there is nothing frivolous or superficial about what you want. It isn't a luxury that can wait until you've taken care of all the 'serious' business of life. It's a necessity. What you want is what you need."

However, the process of changing careers is like quitting smoking, ending a relationship, or grieving a death. Before we can let in the new and feel centered and healthy again, we must let go of the old.

This "letting go" is the first and most difficult part of a career transition. I liken it to going to the dentist. You know your tooth will feel better after the cavity is filled, but you dread the trip nonetheless. Many of us avoid the visit altogether and years later regret neglecting our needs.

With every growth there is a loss. It is essential to teach people that it is normal to grieve a career that no longer suits their needs.

It's also "normal" to feel lost and confused for an extended period of time—sometimes days, months, or even years.

I refer to this period of unknowns as "embracing the void," which is the second major stage of a career transition. Awkward and uncomfortable, this period is crucial to self-discovery. We have to quiet the soul before we can hear its messages; then we need to trust what we hear.

In the final stage of changing careers, which I call "recreating," an integration of old and new takes place and the external world starts to reflect the inner changes of the process. Joy and meaning— the rewards for enduring a career transition—are found here. William Bridges, in his book *Transitions* refers to these stages as "Endings," "The Neutral Zone," and "New Beginnings."

I know from experiencing a career transition myself and from teaching workshops for professionals in work transition that the path is not always straight. We usually go in and out of the letting go, embracing the void, and recreating stages several times during the process of change.

Eventually, through sifting, sorting, and testing our ideas of suitable work, we are able to commit to a new career. Often we receive signals along the way that confirm our instincts about what might be our right livelihood. We may, for example, unexpectedly meet a person joyfully doing the work we are contemplating pursuing or hear a song that inspires us to make a difference in the world. When we embark upon the new career, we may even find that we were not as far from our intended path as we thought, yet the internal upheaval we undertook to reach that discovery can be tumultuous nonetheless.

In the following section, I walk the reader through my two-year process of changing careers from a well-paid high-tech public relations executive to a teacher and coach specializing in transition and a writer of nonfiction, self-help books.

Background/"The Old"

Extraordinary changes are far less likely to happen as long as you lie to yourself or misrepresent the truth about what you really want.

—Robert Fritz, founder of Technologies for Creating

In college I majored in journalism, not knowing what I wanted to do with it except to avoid science and math courses. I've heard similar stories from many adults who haphazardly chose careers.

I remember telling the chairman of the journalism department, a former *Providence-Journal* editor, that I liked to write. "Do you like to write poetry?" he asked, before beginning his account of the reporter's grueling life of long hours and meager wages. "Newsprint is dirty," he told our beginning writing class as he held up a newspaper and showed the smudged type on his fingers.

During the year, he continued trying to weed out the lightweights from the journalism program at the University of Rhode Island. Somehow I survived the cut and moved on to become assistant editor of a new campus magazine. I later became the editor and created an award-winning magazine. The journalism chairman was the faculty advisor, and he had a profound influence on my early career as a newspaper reporter. I sent him clips of my stories that were published in *The Haverhill Gazette* in Massachusetts, where I first worked after college, and he'd return them, marked and edited in red pencil. I got more editing from him as a cub reporter than I ever did from the newspaper staff.

It wasn't long before his grim reporting tales began to ring true in my own life. I resented the pay and the pace, not to mention the difficulty of moving up to a larger newspaper. I entered the field of "trade" journalism, where I worked first at a restaurant magazine,

11

then at a computer newspaper. My love of journalism didn't grow in either position because of the negativity and cynicism I experienced in many people in the profession, so I chose to switch careers.

After giving two weeks' notice, I took a job in public relations (PR)—what journalists refer to as a "flak." As a PR professional in the high-technology industry, I wrote press releases and stories about clients' products and companies, which I then tried to get published in newspapers and magazines or broadcast on TV through telephone persuasion or a carefully written "pitch" letter.

Now I was on the "fast track," working with an up-and-coming agency in Boston. I was twenty-five years old and only the agency's eighth employee and the first female to work on the client side of the business. I had, in fact, joined a boys' club of sorts, working primarily for and with male entrepreneurs. When the company eventually gained national recognition, I prospered with it and became a senior staff member two years later. By then I had traveled extensively throughout the country for press conferences, trade shows, client meetings, and press tours. One night I endured a "red-eye" flight from Los Angeles to Boston. That flight didn't put me to sleep; it woke me up. I knew then what I had suspected for a long while. This lifestyle was not for me. I could no longer emulate the male workaholic model for success. My feminine, creative, and nurturing side had been suppressed too long.

I had no idea what I would do next. I had a journalism degree and a childhood longing to teach. So at age twenty-eight, I (with a journalist friend) started a business that trained companies to build their own PR departments. It was a perfect combination of my interests and skills.

The Monday after I left the Boston agency, I was in business for myself. My partner and I encountered only one problem: There wasn't much of a market for our service. Companies either had their own PR departments or they contracted out for the work. No one really wanted to learn how to build a department. Typically, by the time companies realize they need PR expertise, they are in a crisis, for example, anxious to announce a new product. Playing catch-up and meeting short deadlines is one reason PR is so stressful, not to mention all the client handholding—or "schmoozing"—that goes on. I excelled at the writing and planning components.

So I found myself co-owner of a public relations agency, working with the same types of high-tech clients I had hoped to leave behind. I learned, after spending ten years in the computer industry, that technology has never been, nor will ever be, a passion of mine.

Yet survival needs superseded any other career motives, and the challenge of living on the edge as a successful entrepreneur was briefly thrilling. Besides, letting go of a thriving business that had grown from a startup into a quarter-million-dollar company in less than three years wasn't easy. The financial rewards were plentiful.

I always knew though, that I was meant to do something different.

One day I had the courage to search for it. In January 1990 I sold my high-tech agency, after two years of negotiating with other PR firms and individuals.

I wish I could say the story ended happily there, that there was a roomful of people applauding my decision to start anew. It's often not that way with career transitions.

Switching lifestyles as an adult involves a more intense identity crisis than simply exchanging one mask for another. For me, it involved a lot of internal unraveling to understand how I ventured into jobs with enormous responsibility but little personal satisfaction.

Beginning

Human beings love to say that we love to change. The fact is human beings hate to change. If you fail, it's relatively easy to change because you have no choice. If you have succeeded and need to change, that is the most difficult task of all.

—Lester Thurow, MIT economist

Nobody told me changing careers would be like mourning a death. When I sold my business after two tough years of negotiating its sale, I had a party to celebrate my exit from the corporate PR world. Free at last from responsibility and billable hours, my time to play had come, or so I thought.

I probably held the same illusion of a newly single person just out of a bad marriage. Once out, everything would soon be okay and a new match, or in my case, a new career would appear quickly.

Wrong! Held hostage too long by the demands of the corporate world, without my work, I had no sense of who I was. Before I could begin anew, I had to find myself, which meant peeling away layer upon layer of defenses.

I might as well have jumped from an airplane without a parachute; life without work was that scary. Many other adults who choose to undergo a full-fledged career transition instead of simply changing jobs—and the two experiences are vastly different—are caught off guard. Instead of finding a light at the end of the tunnel, they find themselves at the bottom of a well with a long climb back to the top. Some people, at this point, opt to sabotage the transition rather than endure the uncomfortable moments of recreating a life. I stopped myself from changing my professional identity several

14

times before finally committing to following this process from beginning to end.

A heartbreaking memory flashes back now as I recall my own climb out of the damp, darkened waters. About ten months after I sold my business, I attended a concert with my husband and another couple. My husband and I had been married only two months. "It hurts so bad I want to die," I said to him, while fidgeting in my seat at the concert hall. "I don't know who I am. I can't stand to be around people now."

He had been awakened a few nights earlier by my complaints of an aching stomach. The grief and anxiety from losing an identity that supported me for years caused me physical pain. The hurt in my husband's eyes from his helplessness added to it. I never intended to drag him through this ordeal with me.

Remembering this painful time, I wish someone had told me what I share with you now. These feelings are perfectly normal, and it is possible to move through them and live more joyfully than ever before, but to get through them it takes time—time not easily afforded by our society. You have to create it for yourself.

I spent two years emotionally and financially planning for a career change and another two years of living through the three major stages of transition: letting go, embracing the void, and recreating.

Despite my planning, nothing prepared me for living through an emotional process that challenged every thought I had, and in the end, changed many of my beliefs and reordered my priorities.

Support

The difference between those who fail to achieve their goals and those who succeed is the difference between those who cannot put themselves in a supportive state and those who consistently put themselves in a state that supports them in their achievements.

—Anthony Robbins, *Unlimited Power*

I nudged my puppy out the door that morning, watching her quivering legs touch snow for the first time. With her ears tightly pulled back and terror in her eyes, she ran around in a small circle on our deck, which was laden with two inches of fresh snow, then darted back into the house.

Once inside, she snuggled against my leg and looked searchingly into my eyes for reassurance. After a quick scratch under her neck and a pat on the head, I led her out again. Standing in the wet snow in only a bathrobe and slippers, I encouraged her to explore the snow. She kept glancing up to see if I was there. Slowly she sniffed and romped about, kicking snow in the air, chasing it, and then eating it. Before long—about ten minutes to be exact—I couldn't get her to come back inside.

The fear of the unknown is universal, and for adults in career transition fear is a daily companion. However, unlike my small pup, adults typically don't adjust to new events or circumstances in ten minutes, nor do we always instinctively ask for help.

Assimilating change takes months, or even years. Some, such as laid-off or fired employees, feel like failures, so they isolate themselves. In the end, they create more anxiety and fear by alienating others.

Finding someone to support us through this lengthy process is crucial. A spouse or significant other is not enough because they lack objectivity. Besides, it's too much to expect any one person to provide the encouragement and perspective needed to move through what can become an identity crisis that challenges every one of our resources.

It was helpful for me to check in regularly with at least one other adult who was embarking on a major career change. That connection was the thread by which I felt I was hanging during the initial letting-go stage of my transition.

Support does not come easily unless we look for it. I found connections by reaching out and being honest. I never pretended everything was fine once I left a career in high-tech public relations. I let those I trusted know it hurt a lot to be without work, an income, and a career direction.

About a year into exploring new careers, I joined a group for women in transition. An earlier experience with an entrepreneurs' network had shown me that group support often helps an individual move through difficult times much faster. As people attempting to quit smoking or lose weight know, participating in a support group helps keep us accountable in achieving our goals.

Sharing with others also connects us to the very humanness of being. We learn, for example, that our hurts and fears are not much different from anyone else's. And when we acknowledge our vulnerabilities, they can have less power over our lives.

I Can See Clearly Now

All of our secret hopes come to the surface at the moment when we decide to give up the old and the known. We feel free not only to leap but to allow our daring to spur us on even more.

—David Viscott, *Risking*

The difference between the "haves" and the "have nots" is not money. When I was making $140,000 per year as an executive of a PR agency, I was jealous of the women who were home with their babies. My nature is nurturing and compassionate; the fast-paced technical environments within which I worked crushed my spirit. I knew it, but my mask was comfortable.

Once home, I slowly centered myself. I became a "have."

And in this introspective phase where support was limited, ideas became very clear. The "haves" are simply people who have chosen to follow their hearts and honor their souls. They can be rich or poor, but they are fulfilled. The kind man, who before wallpapering our bathroom, explained that he works slowly but loves his work, is a "have." It showed in his eyes and later in the fine work he did as he matched every pattern perfectly.

My husband is financially successful as a manager of human resources data systems. He is a "have," not because of his paycheck but because he knows how to give himself space to connect with his soul. He has opted to stay a manager rather than target a vice president's slot. Having time to be home, to ride his bike, and to volunteer is as important to him as his work. He is a very happy person.

My husband's childhood friend is a successful businessman who is a "have" for reaching the top. A physical-therapist-turned-entrepreneur, this man operates a sports medicine clinic where his hobbies are his work. His business is successful and so is he. The two reflect one another. The money is there, but it was never the driving force of his success. Helping others will always be a part of this fine man.

My early mentor, the chairman of the journalism department, excelled at his work without ever obtaining a college degree. He is self-taught, which earned him great respect over the years, but he is also very wise. He always pursued his personal interests like canoeing, collecting rare books, reading, and gardening. Even now, in "retirement," he is having lots of fun as proprietor of the Wayside Press, where the art of handset lettering propels his soul. He was always a "have." He used to tell his students that work never seemed like a job to him.

It isn't a "job" to do what you like to do, and taking the time to find "it" can be the most challenging experience of one's life.

The mask is off.

TIPS FOR MOVING THROUGH A CAREER TRANSITION

Patience is a virtue you will now need more than ever.

- Feel your feelings, no matter how painful or varied. Rushing ahead to avoid discomfort is how we sometimes make poor choices.

- Build a support system outside of your relationship with your significant other. Find someone else also enduring a career change.

- Use this time of unknowing and self-discovery to learn to trust your gut and to uncover beliefs about yourself which no longer serve you.

- Take long walks and think about what you loved to do as a child—at age five, eight, or ten years old. Think about your priorities in life and how they might be changing. (Be clear: Do you want the management job for its intellectual challenge or for the prestige of the title?) If you are over fifty, ask yourself, "What is my legacy? What do I want to leave behind?"

- Ask your family and closest friends to name your greatest strengths.

Experimenting

One of the ways people short-circuit transition is by chasing the first impulse that comes along. It's good to keep in mind that impulses are like buses—another one will be along any minute.

—Ross Goldstein, *fortysomething*

Dabbling in a variety of activities—from interviewing as a substitute teacher for a day care center to working at a hot dog stand for a local festival—helped me to explore my inner needs.

I became certified to teach a course called Technologies for Creating™, which is a comprehensive five-week program about developing and achieving creative goals. I trained as an instructor for Project Adventure, which is an outdoor course that uses physical challenge to help build self-esteem.

Each new activity brought further clarification of my career goals. I express myself best when I am helping people. I learned that I prefer to create my own courses rather than teach those developed by others.

Experimenting was my way of moving beyond inertia, even though I was fearful each time I tried something new. I realize it is human nature to be scared. If I, despite my fears—walking along a wire a few hundred feet in the air as part of the Project Adventure training—can transcend fear, so can you. At least try something new before you choose another career.

All dreams begin with a risk.

Stretching

Pushing through fear is less frightening than living with the underlying fear that comes from a feeling of helplessness.

—Susan Jeffers, *Feel the Fear and Do It Anyway*

One winter, during my career transition, I spent two Fridays in training clinics learning to ski backward, move with adaptive equipment attached to my skis, and do wedge turns while blindfolded.

Volunteering to teach handicapped skiing was gutsy. Running a business and moving to a strange city as a cub reporter were my previous contenders for the badge of courage.

With only seven years of skiing skills and no experience working with a physically challenged person, I was terrified. My sixty-nine-year-old classmate, who had been skiing for fifty-five years, and the physical therapist who worked daily with the handicapped, appeared just as nervous. We didn't want to hurt our students.

A love of the outdoors and an urge to help others were early inspirations for my volunteer commitment. Exploring potential careers was another. Yet the determination to keep going, to continue to move beyond my own fears in order to assist another, comes from somewhere deep inside of me. It's the soul, I think, aching to make a meaningful contribution to this world.

Knowing that I had to learn to ski backward in order to guide a student down the mountain enabled me to lose all self-consciousness. It wasn't a matter of "if" I could do it, but rather that I "must" to do it. Volunteering is an extension of self—a calling to reach a higher level of potential.

I refer to this extension as "stretching." When I stretched and gave back to others, I forgot that I was in a legal dispute, recently recovered from major surgery, was renting my condo at a three hundred dollar per-month loss, and had lost a father-in-law, uncle and dear grandfather within a twelve-month span.

In these giving, reaching moments, I remembered instead that I was married to a very kind man who supported my urge to volunteer instead of pushing me to earn a salary.

Deciding to give to someone outside your immediate circle nurtures and inspires the very best of human emotions, often leaving one with a feeling of a natural high for days.

Volunteering was more than self-replenishing for me. It was bonding, too. I may have never met a Federal Express pilot, a commercial fisherman, a respiratory therapist, or an emergency medical technician and realized that we all shared common fears and strengths. Ambition and competition had no place in the unique adventure of helping the physically disabled. In fact, those qualities would be detrimental to the effort. A cooperative team spirit and lots of patience were more essential attributes.

When the ego was dropped, a new will to give of oneself emerged, and volunteering was the best way out of oneself that I came across in thirty-three years. It exceeded all my other addictions—like staying busy and overachieving—that I'd used to avoid dealing with my feelings.

In the stretching, we also increased our self-esteem, not to mention became better skiers.

Vulnerability

As I look back over my life, I consider the times when I seemed to be wandering in the desert, parched of spirit and painfully separated from God. I recognize that I have become much stronger as a result of the spiritual muscle I developed through such trying times. I see that these difficult periods were followed by awakening, spurts of growth, and important changes for the better.

—Alan Cohen, *Joy Is My Compass*

I have wondered many times why we must endure so much pain to receive answers.

Pursuing my curiosity further, I asked our young priest why people often hit "rock bottom" or "give up" before they find God. Those in recovery from dysfunctional behaviors understand this principle well. It's the foundation of Alcoholics Anonymous and other twelve-step programs that support the healing process.

"Until that point, often they have not let themselves feel vulnerable and open," he suggested, adding that the very rich, for example, often insulate themselves.

So much of my work in life has emphasized becoming stronger—taking on the next challenge personally and professionally. I've held responsible jobs, confronted childhood wounds, and moved through uncomfortable situations. The legal dispute over the sale of my business is a perfect example.

"You'll be stronger after this is over," my father reminded me during the ongoing conflict.

Strength is not an issue for me. I've had many bouts with bravery. I'm not sure at any point for the rest of my life that I'll ever have to be as strong again as when I was a fourteen-year-old girl watching my mother lose her mind to schizophrenia and terrorize me in the process.

I've been stretched so far through her mental illness and all the subsequent defenses I developed that there's little elasticity left—which is, in part, how I found myself. I became vulnerable.

It is that way with career transitions, too. One needs to be vulnerable for a while, rather than select a respectable defense, like prestige or income.

However, people often focus on their circumstances and choose their next job accordingly. No one wants to feel unsafe for a period of time. Instead, immediate security becomes the emphasis—like people, afraid of being alone, who end up marrying the wrong person.

In a recent issue of *The Boston Globe*, there was a story about the recession driving people back to school. Most of the adult students weren't sure the extra courses would get them a job, but thought a quick fix of education might help. It may assist a select few. I bet, though, many will still be forced to endure a full-fledged career transition at some point.

Finding work you love isn't the same as looking for a job; it's more about finding yourself. And that discovery doesn't always happen in a classroom. Nor does it happen overnight.

Don't Judge a Book by Its Cover

When you have a purpose, you live your life at another level or in another dimension. You perform out of an inner need. You express your real self. What a joy that releases ...

—Arnold M. Patent, *You Can Have It All*

To the commuters who I passed on the highway while en route to visit a friend, I probably looked liked another successful yuppie driving my luxury Acura sports coupe.

To the neighbors who saw me walking our puppy and watering the garden daily, I probably looked like a bored suburban housewife.

The truth is I am neither of those images. Rather, I am a former executive who has chosen, after a careful search, to become a writer and teacher. During the transitional process I earned $875 for an entire year's work—forcing me to ignore mounting debts while battling with my conscientious, responsible nature.

Had I chosen immediately to attend graduate school or become a mother—instead of recreating my career through self-knowledge and first-hand experience—my external self would have been more accepted and understood.

Yet transitions teach that external symbols are often irrelevant to our internal selves. Rich people aren't necessarily wealthy. Job titles don't determine character. Salaries don't represent worth. Security isn't acquired.

All value comes from within. We give it to ourselves. It's called self-esteem. We get it from expressing who we really are.

25

In searching for our purpose and the subsequent discovery of who we are, the inside pages don't always coincide with the cover.

Tempted

The price one pays for changing goals whenever opposition threatens is that while one may achieve a more pleasant and comfortable life, it is likely that it will end up empty and void of meaning.

—Mihaly Csikszentmihalyi, *Flow*

My redheaded friend from my early reporting days always wanted to be a sportscaster or a deejay. He would have been damn good at it; he had a knack for entertaining, and he loved an audience. I, a bit shy and more reserved, envied his talents. Today, he is a successful PR executive.

I followed in his tracks for many years—not intentionally, but out of fear that there was nothing else for me to do. That fear stayed with me throughout this search for passion, particularly as I saw my life savings vanish.

Each time I liquidated one of my assets to survive this transition, I almost ran back to the frantic life I left.

Two years ago, when I took the first deep plunge into my savings, I thought about finding just one high-tech client to support me in the short term.

In December of that same year, when I had to pay my lawyer a portion of a seven thousand dollar bill, I sold some stock I had carefully invested in hopes of attending graduate school one day. I continued selling off the stock throughout this transition.

One fall—after a course I had spent the entire summer developing and marketing failed to attract any registrants—I borrowed two thousand dollars from my father to pay my lawyer a few more installments on a bill that now exceeded twelve thousand dollars. At the same time, I also called a friend who works at Polaroid, asking him about freelance PR projects. He sent me a package of information, but no work. Thank God! I couldn't even read the press kit. Each technical product description forced my mind to go blank; I didn't want to comprehend that stuff anymore.

Then I registered at a temporary employment agency and scoured the area I lived in for part-time work.

Finally I called a headhunter, who was also a friend of mine. Asking for help has never been easy for me, but when I encountered a one thousand dollar per-month real estate loss due to a vacant condo—on top of the legal fees—I felt humbled. She had no related work available, but told me that most of the growth in Massachusetts was occurring in small businesses, particularly the 1,200 new start-up software companies. She was sure at least one of them would need a PR director.

I thought for an instant again about the financial relief steady employment in the high-tech world would bring. Then I remembered I had done that before, and I had veered so far from my intended path.

"No, Cindy, I have given up everything I have to find work I like," I explained. "To go back to that life now would make this whole pursuit of a new career worthless."

Perhaps, because I had reached the top before, I knew I could build again. Only this time I'm using different tools to reach more centered goals.

Of Time and Timing

I always tell people who train with me that our most important deci-sions are discovered; they're never made ... that we can afford to make the unimportant decisions, but that the real ones we discover.

—Anne Wilson Shaef as told to Laurel King in *Women of Power*

Driving to the hairdresser the other day, I realized that I would probably arrive on time for my scheduled appointment. I knew exactly how long it would take me to get there.

Before I undertook this transition, I had no sense of time other than a feeling of always rushing. I didn't know it took only forty-five minutes to complete grocery shopping. It seemed like it took three hours I didn't have when I moved at my previous frantic pace. I didn't know Christmas decorations that took two hours to put up could be removed in less than thirty minutes. I didn't know it takes one hour to meet my city friend at a twenty-five-mile midpoint because commuter traffic continues throughout the day on major highways.

Now I can almost always tell what time it is without looking at a clock. I live consciously and pace myself accordingly.

In my new awareness, I understand how productivity isn't determined by the number of hours we work. I do my best writing after a few days of solitude or inactivity. I created my first course on changing careers after a winter of teaching handicapped skiing.

I have come to accept that timing cannot be forced. I cannot will an ending to my book any more than I can make my legal dispute disappear. They each will be complete in their own time.

Changing careers has a timing of its own, too. The answer about which direction to pursue may come in a minute or in a year. The length of time it takes to make the discovery has nothing to do with its validity; the waiting is the challenge.

Validation

Self-respect means standing by your deepest truths and knowing your innermost feelings. It means making yourself, and not another, the authority of your feelings.

—Sanaya Roman, *Living with Joy*

No one else's opinion can be worth more than my own ever again. It is a lesson—like many of the other teachings of a career transition—that is easier understood intellectually than lived emotionally.

Society is used to labeling people. Choosing temporarily to explore life without an external identity is threatening to those who live with labels. When I decided to sell my business, for example, few were supportive. "How can you just leave a lucrative business?" one friend asked incredulously. "You're so successful. I don't understand it." Another professional acquaintance warned, "You'll never make that kind of money again."

Explaining to these people that I needed to find more meaningful work before worrying about the financial rewards was fruitless. It was also a turning point for me; I had to follow my heart, regardless of the outcome. Relying on others' approval would be a major setback.

Instead, I became my own best friend. I had to; there was so little understanding from others of the sacrifices, courage, and determination it took to let go of society's expectations and follow my own path.

At first there were cynical remarks. "It's a luxury. Most people can't afford to take time off to see what they really like to do," said an ex-boyfriend who, with his wife, earns in excess of $150,000 a year. Looking back on that conversation, I wish I had told him this: "It doesn't feel like a luxury to be lost and confused for long periods of time and to live without a defined structure and steady income. Rather, it's frightening to travel an unknown, unproven path in the hopes of connecting with my dreams. Every bend in the path feels like an endurance test, and remaining committed to the journey is a constant challenge."

Then there were ignorant comments from people whose perception of change is luck, not choice followed by action. "You're lucky. Not everyone has the money you do," said a woman who had no idea I'd been living without an income for twenty months while incurring legal fees in excess of twelve thousand dollars. I made huge sacrifices, from liquidating all my assets to giving up an identity that was acceptable to and respected by a generation of fast-track, high-achieving baby boomers. Besides, even if I were wealthy, I still would have endured emotional hardships. Changing careers isn't class oriented. Rich or poor, it's about courage—putting your true self on the line. A million dollars cash wouldn't have given me the sense of security I needed to find within.

I do, however, encourage students in my transition classes to be prepared to adjust their financial priorities while searching for their right livelihood. There is hardship and risk involved. Some need to find cheaper living arrangements, spend some of their life savings, and take part-time or temporary work. Others need to work a day job while attending graduate school in the evenings, for example.

Also, the career explorer can expect to feel ultrasensitive and vulnerable for a while. For this reason, I tell my students to be prepared to let go of—if only temporarily, while they complete their search—relationships that are not supportive, which can be as difficult as letting go of a professional identity that no longer supports them.

For me, the worst of these relationships was the green-eyed monster. I confronted this beast everywhere. "It must be nice to sit on the deck and look at the river all day," said one of my husband's friends, who despises his job but is not secure enough to look elsewhere for work he loves. "Is that all you did all day was make this wreath?" said a girlfriend who claimed to understand my exit from the corporate world.

The further I progressed along my path, however, the more my external world started reflecting my inner self, which became stronger each day. A sort of cleansing happened when I lost tolerance for the snide remarks. As a good friend pointed out to me, "Those who are insecure scratch. Those who are secure support." I started choosing to associate with more secure people.

Neighbors who love country living as much as my husband and I do, and who share in the simple pleasures of outdoor labor and the aesthetic rewards of landscaping and gardening, have replaced friends who need constant social activity. Community involvement has become increasingly important, too, for relationships seem to matter more when you live at a slower pace.

My colleagues include therapists, career counselors, and mothers. I value those who nurture others. Solitude and time for reflection are more important to me now than the fast-track perks of prestige and money.

A quiet life is not for everyone, but it is for me, and I'm the only one who can validate that choice. I give myself permission to live the life I love—writing, teaching, coaching, gardening, skiing, biking, and nurturing relationships—even if I have to take an occasional temporary job along the way.

KEY QUESTIONS FOR A CAREER SEARCH

Ponder in solitude and give lots of time to simmer:

• Where have you found the greatest satisfactions in your life? Name five, if you can.

• What motivates you?

• Why are you on this earth? What is your purpose?

• What can you attract through work or a passion that you don't now have in your life?

• Do you have any wounds that could become life gifts? (For example, Mothers Against Drunk Driving [MADD] turned their loss of loved ones into a crusade.)

• How best can you express your authentic self, not the self you were programmed to be by parents or other authority figures? What do you know about yourself that you can share with others? Are you living your dream or someone else's?

• What energizes you and makes you feel alive?

• Is there a path that keeps calling you, even though you may have avoided it for a long time?

• What are your best qualities?

• What brings you the most peace, contentment, and fulfillment?

• Who could mentor you toward a new path?

• Are there any courses that pique your interest?

Solitude

The journey into the light can only be made through the center of darkness.

—Shakti Gawain, *Return to the Garden*

I kept sinking into deep depressions, where letting go of negativity and fear seemed impossible. These energy drainers were so impounded.

My sense of self was seemingly lost, and the choice to retreat to the old ways of overwork seemed saner and safer than risking change once again.

In those scary, lonely moments however, I learned the most about what I needed to change to become a more loving and centered person. It did not matter that I had not learned these lessons earlier, even though I envy those who seem to have caught on quicker and with less pain.

What I did learn was that it matters most that during the dark times—and there are many of them while in a major life transition such as a career change—one stays open long enough to hear the messages. If we repress the hurt and move forward fast, we lose an opportunity for change. I lost the opportunity many times before because I was too afraid to feel vulnerable for so long.

This time, when I finally created the space to change, I stayed with the hurt. My self-esteem was very low, which was obvious in the way I carried myself (poor posture, little eye contact with others, quick and polite conversations that lacked any spontaneity, and a seriousness of spirit).

34

It seems paradoxical, but to make yourself secure you have to feel your insecurities. Feel them, yes, not necessarily show them. That's been my mistake in the past when I've opted to return to safe ways of thinking. I've publicly tried to change, using external events to prod me along. Moving is one way I used to avoid dealing with my shortcomings. Instead of trying to find out why I was unhappy, I kept thinking that once I changed my physical environment everything in my life would improve. Ten moves later, I still felt no better about myself. Promotions and job titles were other defenses of mine. Yet, the more outwardly successful I became, the more inwardly sure I was that something was missing. My true self was buried beneath the layers.

Now, after feeling defeated too much by looking outside for answers, I am selecting solitude as my teacher. It's a much gentler way to gain the insights.

Solitude has taught me that my sensitive inner voice is screeching for expression, which is why I need to write and teach and share myself with others in an intimate open manner.

Living less defensively and more honestly became important too. Sleeping until 10 a.m. some days was a new priority and a great joy. Such rest was the activity I felt most guilty about, having always used work and achievement as a crutch.

I learned to value myself for simply being, not doing. With self-acceptance came acceptance of others, even if their paths differed from mine.

Someone told me that I was a good friend, a good daughter, and a good wife. Her words stunned me—not in their flattery but in my discovery that in just being, I am good. This is a major revelation to me, and it's the foundation of self-esteem. I am enough by being kind, being honest, and being compassionate. All those other activities to which I attempted to attach my identity never changed my core self; they only helped me to hide it.

Well, I didn't want to hide "me" anymore, even if it meant I was "sweet." "Sweet" to me used to mean passive and timid; I tried for a long while to be aggressive and strong. Now, I am just understanding that my strength is my sweet, caring side. I still cringe a bit when I think of myself in this new way, but there is a little girl whom the teachers used to call "Sunshine" who is enjoying her freedom.

It was also through my aloneness—those long nine- and ten-hour stretches until my husband walked in the door—that I discovered the diverse interests and hobbies of my life. They emerged over time, and like a new outfit that one loves and wears well, these new passions came about from trying them on, sometimes many times.

At first I despised the vacant moments, thinking that the faster I filled them up, the better. Baby thoughts came to mind a lot then, but I wisely remembered words of trusted friends and older professional colleagues. "Enjoy some time alone before you have a child. You'll never have that time again," urged a couple we care about and admire. Having raised a puppy since then, I'm glad we listened. Learning to be home in time to let out or feed a dependent ten-week-old whiny pine-colored fuzzball was a huge adjustment for me and my husband; we had been accustomed to coming and going as we pleased for most of our adult lives. A pet's unconditional love is easily worth the tradeoff of caretaking, but it took time to assimilate to the change.

Then a few months later, while working on a freelance project for an architect friend, I told him of my discomfort of the transitional void. He warned, "A lot of women in your position would have a baby right away, but if you do that, you'll just have to confront the question of what you will do for work ten years from now, and it will be even harder then."

In other words, the search for passion doesn't go away. Ever. We're not satisfied until we find it. And no amount of money or number of children can change that.

Bearing the initial wretchedness of solitude after living a frantic pace was torture. A neighbor I met during one of my most fragile moments of this process told me of her experience after exiting the fast track, where she worked as an art broker.

In the beginning, she said, she used to hop a train to the city and visit a museum or watch "Dobbie Gillis" on TV in hiding. Her most dreaded experience—common to nearly all people in transition—was answering the most often-asked question at a cocktail party: "What do you do?" She encouragingly told me however, that as time goes on and you adjust to an undefined period of life, you come to know yourself very well, especially all of your likes and dislikes.

Well, time has passed, and she is right. In addition to learning new skills and avoiding those without any intrigue, I've become acquainted with all my quirks and patterns.

I write better in the afternoon or early evening, at about the time I should be preparing dinner. I suppose that means I enjoy writing more than cooking.

I withdraw from people who lack sensitivity and often feel suffocated by extroverts. I trust slowly, but open easily to those I care about.

I prefer a cold winter evening snuggled in front of a fire drinking a glass of red wine or reading a good book over any party of mere acquaintances.

I used to feel challenged by the "strong, silent types." Now, I'd take a kind, honest exchange any day.

I like people who are genuine, particularly those who are self-aware.

I feel centered and joyful when I attend our new church. The priest balances insight with religion.

I am a homebody who needs to be intellectually challenged. Domesticity must include risks.

I respect my intuition and listen for answers from within. No one knows me and my needs more than I do.

I love the outdoors, especially in the fall.

I also learned a new sense of timing that comes with understanding patience and discipline—skills I lacked on the fast track. Ironically, my lack of patience helped me create a successful business; my lack of discipline helped me resent it. I didn't expect being an entrepreneur would be so hard.

In quietness, new lessons continued to flow. Before, I clogged the dam. In solitude, I learned to value every minute alone.

Signals

When a person is following a path with heart, his or her dreams are usually nourishing, often imparting a sense of well-being. Synchronistically, opportunities seem to open fortuitously, the people we should meet accidentally cross our path, a flow or ease accompanies our work. Each facilitating, unsought event then begins to center a feeling of being blessed, each serving as a lantern along the way, illuminating the path with heart. The sense of fullness and flow influences the sense of time; there seems to be enough time to do whatever we are here for—even parking spaces synchronistically materialize. "Humming along" is a good description of this really good place ... There is generosity and freedom from fear within the psyche and in the world.

—Jean Shinoda Bolen,
The Tao of Psychology—Synchronicity and the Self

I had to take three tests—writing, current events, and spelling— during one of my first interviews for a newspaper job upon graduating from college.

"Secretaries typically spell well," the editor barked at me after scoring my spelling test, in which I received a near perfect score. He never did tell me how I did on the other two exams. He didn't hire me, either.

I always spelled well, even words I could not comprehend or pronounce.

Now, when I meditate, I typically see words instead of pictures. While listening to someone converse, I see the sentence they are speaking before I absorb the content. I love to read. Most writers do. Words are our passion.

In other moments, while walking the beach or hiking in a near-by state park, I recall comments from friends and professional acquaintances telling me I am a good writer.

In fact, no one but me was surprised at my decision to write a book. One former colleague told me I had confronted so many life challenges that I have at least three books in me.

Not wanting to write about news or computers, however, confused me for several years. I hadn't yet written from the soul, where I've learned my passion lies.

In reading books related to career transitions, common themes about finding one's passion emerged. Most suggested the reader recall a dream, a childhood memory, a serendipitous comment or meeting, or a hobby to find a hint about where to find happiness in work. As a six-, seven-, eight-, and nine-year-old girl, I played for hours in my bedroom teaching a make-believe classroom of students. As an adult, I've dreamed of standing in a one-room red schoolhouse, waiting for my students to arrive.

When I decided after beginning this book to also teach classes about the transition process, I was quite unexpectedly given an opportunity to co-facilitate and design a course with a local psychotherapist who had heard me talk about my longing to help those in transition connect with one another. Her offer was a gift from God, because at the time I mistakenly thought I needed a counseling degree to teach my passion. Called "Women in Transition," our class attracted a dozen professionals from the greater Boston area, all of whom rated the course "excellent" in the evaluations.

Later, after teaching on my own for a while, a former student called for advice about switching from a bank consultant's job to a public relations career. During our lengthy conversation, I told her of my dilemma of whether or not to return to graduate school. I thought perhaps additional credentials might help me attract more students for a future course. At the same time, I wanted to be teaching now what I knew about transition, not wait two more years until I completed a master's program.

"I don't think I would have attended your course if you'd had a counseling degree," she said. "I was attracted to your experience of a career transition that you mentioned in your course brochure. The value of the course was its practicality. The fact that you endured a career transition showed me that I could, too."

Living from a sense of meaning and purpose is the reward for enduring a full-fledged career transition. I knew I found my life direction when, after a period of not forcing answers or rushing decisions, I started seeing the same messages in many different places. "You'd be a great inspirational teacher," I recalled my former business partner telling me. "You're an expert on transition. You've taken the time to process all your discoveries and research change," a good friend commented a few months before I began this book. I even started seeing the word "transition" appear frequently in my daily life, particularly when I was about to teach a class.

Others I know have found signs in other ways: they read a book and the line that pops out at them resembles the same thought they had a day or two before; the person they wanted to meet accidentally bumps into them at the grocery store; someone needs their new business service on a day when they have a huge bill to pay; a childhood dream no longer seems far-fetched.

Eventually, the ease and lightness of life replace thoughts of struggle and we career changers sense we have found our path. Then it all seems too easy, maybe even a little fun, and we second guess our choice.

"There's no money in writing," we muse. Other excuses that sabotage dreams sound like this: "My parents would never understand my work as a therapist"; "My colleagues would be shocked if I stayed at home to be a full-time mother"; "I have several college degrees. I can't open a record store even though I love music"; or "I love working with my hands outdoors, but I'd have to retrain all over again to be a landscape architect."

For me, I had to first give myself permission to love my work before I could commit to it. Then I had to trust that it would support me.

Contentment

Happiness is a how, not a what, a talent, not an object.

—Hermann Hesse

Alex was sitting at the back door one morning when our eight-month-old puppy B.J. and I were about to begin our morning routine of fetching the morning newspaper. B.J. greeted him with a press of her dripping pink nose against the door's window, before tossing back her head and shooting me a pleading glance for permission to go out. Those eyes will get you every time; ask any dog owner.

Alex is a ten-year-old black Labrador who lives two houses over. He was our friend. Our backyard became so leveled and worn over one long diagonal stretch of grass that someone once asked if we had an underground irrigation system there. "No, it's Alex's path," we explained.

Alex served as a sage to B.J., showing her how to socialize with the other neighborhood dogs. Luckily, B.J. did not yet pick up Alex's one bad habit of wandering to the main street. Our pup would have been confused by traffic; she spent her young life frolicking amidst open land, with an occasional walk on the beach or through the nearby park.

Watching the two dogs run off in their tiny pack like a father-daughter team, I chuckled to myself at their happiness.

Then I remembered my own.

I love the writing life I had resisted. Mornings are typically composed of a daily check-in with my counselor friend who is also a writer, chores, and errands, and a chance to meet with others if I

41

choose. Afternoons are soul connections when the words just pour from me, sometimes much faster than the sixty-words-per-minute I can type. The technology of the personal computer no longer gets in the way; I write through it.

My favorite room at this point is "the nook," as I have named the office at the back of my house on the second floor, across from the room that I hope one day is a nursery. Beside the alcove that makes me feel like a little girl tucked in bed with a warm blanket, a cup of hot chocolate, and a good book, sit my PC, laser printer, heaps of books, pictures, awards, and other memorabilia that bring me joy.

One wall features a bulletin board full of quotes. Many of the quotes I selected from those items found on the horoscope page called "Reflection for the Day" in *The Boston Globe*. As an entrepreneur, one of my favorites is: "Luck is not something you can mention in the presence of self-made men," from E. B. White. When I was developing my course for adults in career transition, I clipped this one: "You can waken men only by dreaming their dreams more clearly than they can dream them themselves, not by demonstrating their lives as geometrical theorems are demonstrated," from Alexander Herzen. In the beginning of my own career transition, during the time I slept long hours, I liked the following: "An intellectual improvement arises from leisure," by Samuel Johnson.

There were three other quotes I jotted down, without knowing their source. I found these especially helpful during my legal dispute. The first my counselor friend Gail passed on to me. It says, "Serenity isn't freedom from the storm, but peace amidst the storm." I am unsure of where the other two came from. One says, "Security is not having things; it's handling things." The other claims, "We develop a joyful attitude when we remember that challenges are temporary."

One of the first quotes I ever tacked to the board, which I like as much today as I did when I started my first business, is this: "The people who get on in this world are the people who get up and look for the circumstances they want, and, if they can't find them, make them," from George Bernard Shaw.

Drawing on less substantiated wisdom, a recent horoscope for Leo is what I have pasted to my computer terminal for inspiration these days. It reads, "After a brief time-off period, you come back stronger than ever. Use your power to help others as well as yourself. Your words carry extra dramatic force and appeal."

Manifesting

A journey is a person in itself; no two are alike, and all plans, safe-guards, policing, and coercion are fruitless. We find after years of struggle that we do not take a trip; a trip takes us.

—John Steinbeck

I end this section of the book feeling peaceful, centered, and hopeful. The pieces of the puzzle are reassembled and my life is a blend of commitments that reflect my true and best self.

I created a new business, guiding others through transition. My students are adults like myself who are pursuing long-lost dreams. Many have been successful at living others' dreams; now they're ready to untap their own. It's exciting to watch their new lives unfold.

Interest in my courses grows steadily and at a controlled pace, which suits my more reflective lifestyle. I also continue my one-on-one coaching with adults who are changing careers, starting or growing businesses, restructuring relationships, or seeking to improve the overall quality of their lives.

I continue my inspirational writing, working simultaneously on a second book about relationships. Committing to manuscript the writings of an inward journey solidifies a life purpose. I am meant to share myself with others. The written word helps me stay open and more intimately connected to my clients and myself.

Quality is a priority in my work and in my relationships. I pre-fer teaching a few students who are committed to change rather than a crowded classroom of adults looking for quick and easy answers. The financial rewards are less lucrative, but the emotional satisfaction is far greater. A sense of meaning and a feeling of being connect-ed to my soul are payoffs, not tradeoffs.

ACTION ITEMS FOR THE CAREER EXPLORER

Take initiative and move beyond fear. We are rewarded when we act.

• Get your career tests done by a qualified career counselor, through a community college, or on the Internet. Myers-Briggs, the Strong Interest Inventory, and the Campbell Skills and Interest Inventory are three of the best tests that can help pinpoint your strengths and interests.

• Experiment with the many options the career tests will provide for you. Don't necessarily choose the quickest solution. The career that can serve you over the long haul may take hard work upfront to implement.

• Volunteer for a cause you believe in and/or take on temporary job assignments through an agency specializing in placing temporary employees. Both activities will keep you motivated and connected with others.

• Do something creative like taking an art class, planting a garden, learning a new computer program, or building a dollhouse.

• Read *Transitions* by William Bridges and *Callings: Finding and Following an Authentic Life* by Gregg Levoy.

My friends and professional acquaintances share the same standards of excellence, integrity, and goodness. Mutual support and warmth are also at the foundations of these relationships.

Here I begin yet another transition. As I finish this section of my book, I will be a new mother. The tiny being who kicks within reminds me of life's miracles.

I encourage all of you who want to walk a different path to find the courage and support to do so. Stay committed to a vision of finding work you love. You don't have to know what the work is, but you need to believe you will find it. Thinking long-term is crucial. If you focus on the day-to-day problems—like lack of money, loneliness, and undefined time—you will get stuck in your circumstances. Dreams move us forward.

Begin by uncluttering your life. Make a list of your priorities. Discard those activities from your life that don't support your dreams. For ideas on how to identify and release serenity stealers read the book *The Power of Positive Choices* by Gail McMeekin.

Once you've cleared your head, and hopefully some time on your calendar for exploring, stay open, be patient, and remember: like the twist of a kaleidoscope, new images are formed slowly. Trust the process, even when it seems a little blurry.

II. BECOMING A MOTHER

Introduction

Of all the things I've learned to do in life, mothering is among the most difficult. Just when you think you've got it all figured out, your child enters a new stage or backslides into an old one.

—Susan Bernard, *The Mommy Guide*

As a teacher and life coach, I once focused part of my business on guiding women through the transition into early motherhood. Later, I expanded my course offerings to include workshops for helping women move beyond motherhood and reclaim parts of their identities that were lost in the care-taking needs of their families.

Through my work I've noticed many common themes. One is that women have difficulty acknowledging their mothering gifts. They know mothering is important work, but when asked to describe their strengths and contributions, many women come up shorthanded. My second observation is that mothers who stay at home full time feel a loss of self-esteem. Many women rightfully grieve that the worldly creatures that they were (before children) vanished when their days got reduced to a five-mile radius, centered around a young child's life.

I've spent the past eight years teaching these women—new mothers and the more experienced ones who are now looking for fulfillment outside of the home, too—that it is the way our contemporary society structures the role of the mother that makes it so difficult for women to feel whole, secure, and connected in this sacred work of raising children.

To begin with, women are given no pay and little recognition for their work as mothers. Ironically, we—who so many people depend on to efficiently manage a family—are termed "dependents" if we choose to stay home with our children.

Instead of supporting women in their critical new roles, our society all but abandons us from the very beginning. Many health insurers rush new mothers out of the hospital within twenty-four hours of giving birth. At this point, many women cannot even move about or sit comfortably, never mind provide round-the-clock care for a newborn. Then we leave many of these women home alone without the guidance of extended families of bygone eras. Even if women have spouses fortunate to work for companies that offer paternity leaves, most men are not encouraged to take the time off.

When mothers come together in groups and see their commonalities, their dissatisfactions are depersonalized.

Becoming a mother is the most significant transition in a woman's life. Every choice a woman makes from the moment she accepts a child through birth or adoption has the potential to impact another human being. What an awesome responsibility!

Moreover, mothering involves multiple transitions. Mothering a newborn is different from mothering a preschooler. Guiding a first grader is different from supervising a fifth grader. Parenting a teenager changes us once again.

"My husband has had the same job his entire career," one mother tells me. "I have been at home full-time when the kids were little, worked part-time when they started school, and now am entering the workforce full-time. My husband hasn't had to continually restructure his life like I have."

Complicating matters, many of us were not even clued in about the depth of the motherhood transition by our closest friends and relatives, so we think we're doing something wrong when we find the constant nurturing of an infant to be challenging and lonely. *The truth is there is so much more to this mothering business than nurturing children.*

Here are some examples from my life: enduring an excruciating twenty-hour labor and worrying about the health of my new baby, who was so overstressed that she was rushed to an oxygen tent and the nurse asked my husband if he'd like to call in a priest; learning how to finagle a car seat, hold a baby bottle, mix formula, and soothe a cranky baby at the same time; accepting the hormonal-induced mood swings of a body readjusting to a non-pregnant state; attempting to work part-time with a crying baby in the background; and finding reliable childcare relief.

I remember my early days at home with a newborn, feeling lonely because I didn't have a "mother" with whom to share my experience. I will always envy women who had a mother to lean on at the beginning of the motherhood journey, for what I've come to understand is this: Every mom I once judged to be calmer than me had nannies, mothers, and/or mothers-in-law or other relatives to give them breaks on a regular basis from constant childcare responsibilities.

Many women without relatives nearby have echoed my feelings of loneliness as they, too, learned their new caretaking role in isolation.

"If we really knew all this, there would be zero population growth," joked one new mother learning to juggle a second child. Her friend, a lawyer for one of New York's most prestigious law firms, agreed. "This is the hardest job I ever had," she said.

Many of us cling to the childrearing books from the pediatric experts like Dr. Penelope Leach and Dr. T. Berry Brazelton, read *What to Expect When You're Expecting* and *What to Expect the First Year,* and hope that our newfound friend at the playground will know more about mothering than we do. Later, many of us discover that playground chatter does not fulfill our need for intellectual stimulation, and sometimes we feel lonelier when we leave our outing than when we arrived.

The "secrets" no one passed on to us—that childbirth can hurt; that mothering is stressful, lonely, and even boring sometimes; that roles change, friendships shift, and marriages wobble through an unsettling period after a child enters a family—don't fit in with the angelic-looking mother in the Gerber baby commercials.

What we need to be taught, instead of a false image of constant serenity, is that mothering is indeed the hardest job there is. There are no rules or structures for defining your days, there are no boundaries establishing when you have given enough or too much of yourself to another human being, and in the long winter months or days home with a sick child, sometimes there is no adult connection.

Gail Kauranen Jones

In the following section, I walk the reader through my journey into motherhood, from infancy to pre-teen. As I evolved through this transition, I came to know quite clearly that no woman is "just" a mother. We are guides for life, and the better nurtured and support-ed we are, the more gifts we can bestow on our children.

Baby Blessings

The most common fallacy among women is that simply having children makes one a mother—which is absurd as believing that having a piano makes one a musician.

—Sydney J. Harris, *A Mother's Journal*

"There's no way you can't believe in God after experiencing the birth of a child," my father once told me. My father always loved children, but it was the miracle of a third person created from two that he was in awe of.

Twice, I was fortunate to not only witness, but to participate in, that same miracle. I gave birth to my daughter, Caitlin "Catie" Elizabeth, October 20, 1992, and my son, Brendan Patrick, October 13, 1996. The four-year age span and the gender difference allowed me to witness the miracles in different ways. My daughter talks all the time, but mostly softly. I've nicknamed her "the babbling brook." My son is often quiet, but when he cries, he yells. He's more like a loud alarm clock.

Even their births were dramatically different. My daughter nearly died following my grueling "natural" labor. "It's like trying to get a piano through a keyhole," one of my friend's mothers once said. That description seemed accurate to me in giving birth to my daughter.

My mother-in-law, who was anesthetized through all four of her children's births, told me, "Giving birth is easier than going to the dentist." I'm not sure I agree with that assessment, although during my son's birth, following an epidural injection I insisted on having,

I laughed through contractions that surely would have had me gasping for breath at my daughter's birth.

The unique qualities of my children vary, too, but their presence in my life has one certainty: My children changed me forever, in most ways for the better.

They've blessed me with their tenderness and innocence, challenged me with their testy growth spurts.

Before children I braved many adventures, including skiing in Alta, Utah, by myself, when I had never touched deep powered snow before. Since my children's births, my world narrowed, which sometimes meant I didn't leave the five-mile radius of home for months.

When I was single and shortly after I married, I vowed I'd never lose myself in my children, even though I consciously chose to be an at-home mother. I'd keep my interests alive, my friendships intact, my intellect challenged. The intent all sounds good on paper. Then a child gets a double ear infection that lasts for weeks, you haven't slept more than two hours a night, and the thought of meeting that intriguing friend for dinner is not appealing. A nap on the couch becomes the preference.

Recovered from sickness and insomnia, I decided to do some freelance work to keep my creative juices flowing. The problem was that the people I needed to interview didn't always return my calls when my baby was napping; sometimes they called back when the baby was screaming to be fed.

Frustrated by trying to do it all, we are tempted to give up. Some women return to the paid work force; others choose full-time mothering. The part-time balance is, for most mothers I know, a myth. Two part-time jobs, mothering and paid work, create more stress and are more time-consuming than one full-time position.

Baby blessings don't come with any directions.

A Daughter's Sadness—Mothering from a Void

Parenting often doubles as self-parenting when a mother still longs to be mothered.

—Hope Edelman, *Motherless Daughters*

The workshops I teach for mothers incorporate the same set of skills I use in the workshops I teach for professionals in transition. I believe mothers have the most difficult job there is, and that we as a society need to help raise the status of mothers—giving women who do the job well the same privileges professionals receive, such as recognition, salaries, and paid time off. At the very least we need to help mothers build career paths that enable them to realistically nurture both themselves and their families. The Superwoman model, the ideal mother who simultaneously excels in a demanding fast-track job, is a myth, one that leads to burnout, not success. Most women I know are looking for a saner quality of life. Even women who have broken the glass ceiling have acknowledged the toll that the climb took on their relationships.

Can you imagine seeing a mother selected as *Time* magazine's "Person of the Year" because she balances caring for her children with taking care of herself? Or because she helps a disabled child learn to walk or a shy child stand up in front of a crowd or an academically slow child reach great achievements?

I do dream such dreams, because helping women honor themselves as mothers and as human beings is one of my life's passions. I came upon my passion in one of the ways I teach others who are looking for a purpose or meaning to life. I returned to the most wounded part of me and turned my adversity into healing.

You see, it's quite paradoxical that I, who lead mothers to discover themselves, grew up a good portion of my life motherless. I saw my own mother, who in high school was voted "most likely to succeed," crumble first under the pressures of parenting, then later under the terror of schizophrenia.

I couldn't heal my mother or even help her achieve a slight fraction of the quality of life portrayed in the movie "A Beautiful Mind," based on a true story about a schizophrenic who goes on to win a Nobel Prize.

Yet I have a choice about how to live my life. Part of that choice is trying to make sure no woman is abandoned by neglect and left in isolation like both my mother and I were. My mother has a brain disease that alienates and scares people, including me, sometimes. For a long time, I was ashamed of her disease, and that kept me in hiding too.

Mothers need to connect with one another and share their stories, even the sad ones. We learn from our vulnerabilities. Following is a glimpse of my deepest hurt, which I have spent my entire adulthood trying to heal.

* * *

A good friend of mine, confronted with a difficult in-law at her wedding, said to me on what should have been a joyous day, "Every rose has a thorn."

I've recalled that saying many times since and have seen its truth. Three weeks after my husband and I became engaged, we attended his father's funeral. The sale of my successful business was thwarted by a lawsuit. The three years of serenity I found in my country condominium later became ten years of financial loss.

We're always balancing joy and sorrow, gain and loss, as we hope that the good times will eventually outweigh the bad. As I mature, I continue to seek ways to turn misfortune into opportunity, at least an opportunity to learn one of life's significant lessons.

The birth of my daughter was one such example of how I learned to juggle my conflicting emotions. While her arrival marked one of the happiest days of my life, it also untapped in me an intense sadness in the months that followed as I realized for the first time the significance of the loss of my own mother.

My mother began exhibiting signs of schizophrenia when I was fourteen years old, which began with irrational comments such as that the TV was talking to her or the Martians were coming. This abnormal behavior progressed to the point where she taped up all the wall sockets, kept all the shades pulled down throughout the day, and refused to answer the phone. Eventually she tried to kill herself, which led her to the first of many psychiatric wards.

The catatonic woman who lies on a couch all day smoking cigarettes in no way resembles the person who gave birth to me.

My mother's withdrawal from life's responsibility—although not purposeful—has been quite hurtful. To put it quite simply, my mother doesn't love me the way most mothers love their daughters. My mother loves from a diseased mind, where she is not held accountable for any of her actions. I became a super-responsible adult as a direct result.

Even after a grueling labor and hours of not knowing whether my daughter was going to live or not, I was never asked by my mother how I felt. My mother looked at my baby, but she didn't offer me a hug, a kiss, or even a word of encouragement about the mothering journey on which I had just embarked. Even co-workers from my husband's job sent flowers and a card.

Two months after my daughter's birth, my husband severed two fingers in a snow blower accident. I was up every two hours with a nine-week-old baby and a husband in agonizing pain. My mother did not offer to bring a meal or provide an hour of childcare relief. I felt no support.

I learned mothering by *doing* mothering, by reading every child-care book and taking every parenting course time could afford. Sadly, many women today are learning mothering that way. We don't have the support of community and extended family like other generations. Fast-track careers sometimes take precedence over parenting. Most corporations don't support families, despite the media stories to the contrary. Just ask my husband, who was called at the hospital during the delivery of our daughter with a question about work. Later, he was directed to return to work, although he had scheduled a two-week vacation around her birth.

Compounding the lack of maternal support in my life now, I also feel a deep hole inside me from all those horrific years I endured as a teenager. While I've spent much of my adult life healing and filling the void (which was a full-time job in itself for a long while), I continue to feel this lack in the simplest moments of my life.

Each time I snuggle with my daughter or comfort her, I wonder how much calmer I would feel during adversity had someone consoled me instead of threatening or ignoring me. Each time my child tries a new activity, like riding a bike or taking a dance class, I wonder if I would have played more as an adult had I been encouraged to explore more.

I know that in raising a daughter I need to be aware that a girl's self-esteem often plummets in puberty. My daughter will need attention from me and my husband even more during those trying times, yet, it was during that critical junction of adolescence that my mother exited my life. What would I have been like if my mother had watched me play tennis when I was number one at singles in high school?

Since becoming a mother, I've done a lot more entertaining between my daughter's christening, birthday parties, and play-groups. My husband and I also seem to play host on most of the holidays, yet I don't remember my mother ever entertaining guests in our home. In fact, most of the meals I recall came from a can or a freezer package. Social graces, proper etiquette, cooking tips, and housekeeping skills were not taught to me. The only neighbor I remember in our home was the policeman next door who had to force my mother to the floor, throw her in a straight jacket, and bring her by paddy wagon to the local mental hospital.

Needless to say, I don't take having guests in my home for granted. I usually make a big, stressful ordeal of the situation, even though I love having a home to which my daughter can bring her friends and their parents. I've trembled through many an elaborate party (particularly in my former career as a PR executive), unsure of what to say, where to sit, which fork to eat with, or even what the food in front of me was.

Shopping excursions are another example of a simple event that causes me great pain. Every time I see a mother and daughter with a baby in a stroller, walking the mall or eating lunch at a restaurant, I feel the emptiness again. I am reminded of the day I picked out a beautiful wedding gown. I asked my mother if she would like to see it. I spent an hour and a half driving to pick her up, bringing her to the bridal boutique, then returning her home—one of the loneliest ninety minutes of my life. At the bridal shop, the owner arranged the dress, so my mother could see it hanging, before helping me slip into it. You know those little-girl dreams of wanting to feel like a princess in a wedding gown? That's what I wanted to feel that moment when

I walked out for my mother to see. Instead, I stood frozen as she said nothing. Not one word. Even the storeowner shook her head in dismay. I kept harping at my mother, "What do you think, Mom?" Eventually, she answered, "The train is too long." Not even a tiny suggestion that I may have looked pretty or seemed happy—just a criticism. I dropped my mother off at her home and cried all the way back to my condominium. I didn't buy the dress, a decision I later regretted; the memory of that moment was just too painful.

There were many other basic skills and courtesies I wasn't taught that caused me many moments of excruciating embarrassment during my teenage and college years. One example was proper etiquette about bringing a hostess gift. I often showed up as a guest, empty handed, not from lack of appreciation, but from ignorance. I also dressed improperly for different occasions—particularly baby and bridal showers and often times even work—not understanding the rules of proper attire. Once I showed up at my corporate job in a red shoulder-bearing dress. A kind secretary suggested I wait to wear the dress next time on a date. After that, I was sure to buy suits, and often I overpaid, just to be sure they were right. I alternated between talking too deeply about soul matters to casual company and not talking at all in a social or business situation.

Having endured so many awkward and often shameful moments, I value two things greatly in other people: kindness and acceptance. My daughter will know these values, I think. My circle of adult friends is more inclusive and varied than that from my childhood acquaintances. And I keep extending the circle to gentler folk, who live from an internal set of values.

I continually try to parent my daughter well, while being conscious not to overcompensate for my shortcomings. It's another juggling act for me. Only, unlike my mother, I am accepting responsibility for my mothering role. Part of that responsibility is embracing my own sadness. It's my story, not my daughter's. Had my mother physically died I would have been given permission to grieve a long time ago. Something I understand now that I, too, am a mother, is the fact that she is alive makes the sorrow of her loss even more painful.

I don't get—and probably never did receive too much of—what I give to my daughter, and that mother nurturing is not replaceable. It's not something my husband, my child, my friends, my colleagues, my other relatives, my work, or my hobbies can give me. It's gone. I am now learning to mother myself.

FOR MOTHERLESS MOTHERS

Break the chain of hurt and/or rejection.

• Whether you lost your mother through death, divorce, physical or mental illness, or abuse, you need to grieve the loss. Even if your mother passed away twenty years ago or she checked out from being involved in your life five years ago, if you have never expressed the grief, it is still within you. You may avoid feeling it through workaholism, constant anxiety, or by continually changing residences, jobs or other external circumstances. You cannot run from it; it will catch up with you.

• Read the book *Motherless Daughters* by Hope Edelman.

• Understand that when you became a mother you may have experienced more anxiety or even depression than other mothers who were well-nurtured. Be kind and compassionate to yourself. Seek professional help if you need it; reaching out is a sign of health, not weakness.

• Give yourself a second childhood. Play with your children in the ways you may not have been able to experience. Jump on that seesaw, cruise down a slide, kick your heels high in the air on a swing, make homemade playdough, drink hot chocolate, and have "jammie days" when you sit on the floor and do puzzles snuggled next to your kids.

• Look for mother mentors. Hire a "doula" to help with the caretaking of your new baby, or ask a friend to ease you into your motherhood role.

• Trust your instincts. Repeated studies have shown that adults who were abandoned in childhood are highly intuitive because they had to be ultra-alert and knowing as they fended for themselves.

• Accept that no one can ever make up to you that lost childhood. Stop looking for a mother in your relationships and learn to mother yourself. Positive self-talk is a great beginning. Talk as gently and kindly to yourself as you do to your newborn. Give yourself a hug after a stressful day.

• Know that beside the deep aching hole you may feel within your heart or in the pit of your stomach is a power greater than yourself to guide you always. Any time you feel lost in that abandonment wound, breathe deeply from the abdomen and ask for grace. Help will come forth.

Self-Doubt

It's a myth that mothering comes naturally. We don't celebrate the uncertainty of parenting. It's an ongoing role of incompetence.

—Judith Jordan, the Stone Center at Wellesley College.

I've always wanted to be a mother. In my teenage years, not understanding fully how much work was involved in raising human beings, I envisioned having ten children. Even in my twenties, when I was successful professionally, there was no doubt that when I had children I would make mothering them a priority over any paid career.

When my daughter Catie was born, I chose to be what is now referred to as an "at-home" mother. Regardless of whether I do paid work or not, I am judged by our paternalistic society as a homemaker and immediately devalued for being "just a mother"—even in the 1990s and 2000s, when we're supposed to be so liberated.

On the bad days—and there have been many, especially during the ear-infection-driven winters and the morning "I won't get dressed" power struggles with a strong-willed two-year-old—I wonder if my being home is best for my daughter. I know it's not always best for me. The isolation, lack of intellectual stimulation, and tight financial restrictions test the best of us. Yet, I selected to make the self-sacrifice in hopes of raising a more secure child. Each time I thought I had had enough of living within a house strewn with toys, watching "Sesame Street," and listening to the nonstop chatter of my little one, I'd research a daycare situation. Then, when I saw the children napped on floor mats, I opted to keep my daughter at home. I wanted my child to feel the warmth of napping in her own crib, even though daycare workers and parents who use these facilities tell me the children adapt quite well and even like sleeping on floor mats.

Now that my daughter is in preschool and loves telling me about her rest times, I bet they were right. Still, Dr. Brazelton's recommendation of raising children at home, if at all financially possible, for at least two years, still rings in my ears. Even now when I'm sick or tired, I like to rest in my own bed. It comforted me to offer Catie the same thing.

Mothers with two or more children tell me that they are not as willing to make the same self-sacrifices they did with their initial child with their second. It's self-preservation, I suspect. You can't keep giving if you don't give to yourself. The well needs to be replenished.

I'm getting to know the exact moments when my well has run dry. I get short tempered and angry—something I believed a well-intentioned, educated, and self-aware mother could control. In those moments when I lose it—yell at the child I promised myself I would never raise my voice to—I think my daughter would be better off emotionally if I let someone else raise her.

Then I need to remind myself to keep counting to ten, one hundred, or even more, before yelling, and find a way to re-channel my frustrations. I work out three days a week, continue to look for ways to stay intellectually challenged, and address the underlying rage about the ways in which our society devalues mothers.

I have yet to find a mother—and I'm surrounded by many through my work—who thinks she does this job superbly on a daily basis. It doesn't help that we're not given any feedback or positive reinforcement, never mind a paycheck or yearly vacation. I often hear comments from someone who has seen my husband with my daughter at the playground or in the grocery shop. Their remarks range from "He is so good with her" to "He is a super dad."

No one has told me I am a good mother. Yes, I'm often more harried with my daughter than my husband is, but I've spent twelve hours with her—not two. Like other children, my daughter does most of her behavioral testing with me, because I am her mother, her safe place to learn limits.

I'm starting to understand that not being acknowledged for my mothering skills and contributions doesn't mean I'm a bad mother. Even the "down" moments that are less than perfect don't mean I failed.

There are no standard rules for motherhood. Some mothers who are naturally patient are well suited to at-home mothering. Other mothers may need to hire a nanny early on for their own sanity and that of the child. All mothers need to give themselves permission to seek relief from ongoing childcare. Back-up support benefits both the mother and the child.

My self-doubt reminds me I have to be gentler to myself and give myself the nurturance, encouragement, and support that our society doesn't provide for mothers—yet. If my daughter becomes a mother within my lifetime, I will be by her side, assuring her that this is indeed the most difficult job there is. If she chooses to mother full-time, she better be prepared to pat herself on the back and find the validation from within. I'm still working on it. It's as tough a daily challenge as surviving the terrible twos.

Caught between Two Worlds...
A Glimpse at Secondary Infertility

The desire to perpetuate the parenting role is generally more character-istic of mothers than fathers ... While a woman may mourn the poten-tial loss of future children, her husband may grieve for the more imme-diate loss of his wife whom he feels has changed.

—Harriet Fishman Simons, *Wanting Another Child*

Of all the transitions I endured in my thirty-eight years of life, nothing prepared me for the bad news on that Friday, October 13* of all days. My husband and I were told by one of the region's leading infertility specialists that our chances of conceiving another child naturally were one in one thousand. Our daughter Catie was, in fact, a statistical miracle. Based on earlier test results of which we weren't aware of at the time, the likelihood of her arrival without external assistance was slim.

"At least you have one child already. You should be grateful for that," is the universal message everyone tells the couple of single children. (Please note the word "single" instead of "only"; "single" is an amount, while "only" implies lack).

I felt gratitude every time I looked into my daughter's eyes—and knew at a deep level that my life and my husband's were touched by grace. I still felt an intense sadness, similar to the pain of grieving the loss of a loved one.

What many others have difficulty understanding—and only those enduring the devastation of secondary infertility seem to com-prehend—is that not being able to have another child is a huge loss.

60

I lost two things: a choice and a dream. I wouldn't have chosen a single-child family—even though my research shows the stigmas of "spoiled only children" are often false. Many single children are high-achieving, well-adjusted adults. My dream was a family of four. For years I had a picture of two towheads sitting on leaves plastered to my office wall. After already experiencing pregnancy, childbirth, and the warm snuggles and fresh baby smells of a newborn, I felt my loss even more. I loved being pregnant.

And while adoption and advanced fertility technologies could bring us another child or even two (there's a 25 percent chance of having twins with in vitro fertilization), I wasn't sure I could follow either of those paths. I still needed to grieve my loss.

In fact, my daily challenge was to balance my feelings of gratitude for my daughter with permission to grieve. Resolving infertility takes time—time not easily afforded to a thirty-eight-year-old woman. If my husband and I chose the technological route, we needed to be conscious of my ticking clock. Thirty percent success rates can drop to 4 percent over a two-year period. If we chose the adoption process, we needed to carefully monitor the resources required for pursuing this option over the time and money we provide for our existing child. Did we use our limited family time to prepare background checks and home studies for social workers? Did we forfeit our daughter's college education fund to bring another child into our family?

These were not easy questions to answer, especially when weighed against the needs of our three-year old. I wanted to spend her young years nurturing her. I had put my career aspirations on hold to be there for her. Do I toss my precious time alone with my daughter aside in a relentless pursuit of another child?

Or put another way, how many moments of the present was I willing to miss in hopes of the future? My daughter's childhood was passing quickly.

If I accept our current family size, how do I answer my child's request for a sibling? How do I deal with the sadness every time parents and teachers talk about "children" in the plural sense? Or the loss I feel when I watch my daughter mimic breastfeeding by placing one of her dolls to her chest and I wish I could let her observe a real baby feeding from her mom?

When do I stop saving my daughter's clothes for another child? When do I stop hoping each month that we'll beat the odds and conceive another miracle?

When is enough enough? Does acceptance of a single child come, or do we who experience secondary infertility carry this sadness with us throughout our lives like we do the loss of a loved one?

And if we make the choice to move on, is it possible to look back without regret that we didn't follow through on all options?

Harriet Fishman Simons says in her book, *Wanting Another Child: Coping with Secondary Infertility,* that those experiencing secondary infertility are caught between two worlds: those of the infertile and those of the fertile. As a result, couples with secondary infertility feel quite isolated. They don't receive the empathy of those who are infertile and they live in the parenting world of the fertile, experiencing babies on a daily basis.

Surprisingly, between 50 and 70 percent of American women experience secondary infertility according to Simons, yet less than 30 percent of those experiencing secondary infertility seek help. Many don't even know they have a problem. Some just assume that because they have one child they will have another.

Perhaps, given the magnitude of the issue, ignorance is bliss. I've never thought harder about any issue in my life. As difficult as it has been, I've also never opened up easier or connected so well with others in a similar situation. I have found that while others experiencing secondary infertility can't give me the answers I seek— those will have to come from within, in their own time—these other mothers give me instant understanding. We know we each live on an emotional seesaw of cherishing the child we have and grieving the one we want.

---

* My son was born exactly one year later, on October 13, 1996, without any outside medical intervention. The miracle of his birth reminds my husband and I that during our most difficult life challenges nothing is impossible.

Summer Blues

The role of mother is a high-stress job in itself. The assumption has been that because mothering is supposed to come naturally to women, it's somehow easier than their other roles. That's not necessarily so.

—Rosalind Barnett,
Wellesley College Center for Research on Women

Summers are definitely the hardest season for at-home mothers of young children, particularly for those of us who've had the luxury of a few morning hours off while our little ones were in school or napping.

There is simply no "downtime." This summer, with a four-year-old and a nine-month-old, I was lucky if I could shovel in a spoonful of blueberry yogurt for lunch standing up at our kitchen counter or munch a raw peach en route to yet another errand.

I remember one particular summer as being the worst. It began with a summer vacation—our two-week family retreat to our rented beach house in the dunes off Eastham Bay on Cape Cod. The tiny oceanfront cottage I found a few years ago while walking the National Seashore, our hideaway, was not only discovered, but it was sold right out from under our feet. During the first week of our desperately needed vacation, the realtor called to say a prospective buyer was coming to look at our cottage. That buyer came the same morning my four-year-old daughter woke up with a severe case of chicken pox.

I drove to one of those roadside T-shirt stands to buy an inflatable pool so my daughter could take an oatmeal bath. The cottage only had a shower. Due to its large size, the pool had to be placed outside on the sand. My daughter refused to bathe while realtors and potential buyers were in full view of her naked body.

While the entourage toured our cottage, I sat outside in the sand with my crying child, counting the minutes that seemed like hours, until we were alone. Being alone was something I didn't have on this vacation.

When they finally left, I soothed my daughter by sleeping in her tiny bunk bed with her. Over the next several days we were visited again by the realtor, the building inspector, the fire department, and the current owners. By the middle of the second week our cottage had been sold.

My two friends from college who rented beach houses nearby with their families were around a lot, too. My father also spent two days with us. Had I felt rested, I would have enjoyed their company. Instead, I felt stressed from lack of respite.

The end of vacation was a relief and a lesson. Family vacations are not "time off" for moms unless there is relief from continual childcare. My vacation was simply doing my job in a different locale with different people around. Even my husband, who previously traded off time alone with me, could not offer any relief. Our infant son was teething, and he needed as much cuddling as his itchy older sister. We each spent our vacation taking care of one of our children.

Our return home went smoothly—for about a week. Then, one Thursday evening while I was making dinner, I heard my daughter fall while running to her toy room. "Gail, I think you better come over here," my husband sternly said. As I walked over to the other side of the family room I saw my daughter huddled in a ball, with blood gushing from the top of her head. I ran to grab a cloth and ice and ordered my husband, who was standing by, looking lost, to call the doctor.

Funny how husbands assume wives know what to do in a medical emergency. I was trained as a journalist, not as a nurse or doctor. I knew no more than he how to handle this, but it was relegated to "Mom" nonetheless.

Ten minutes later I was sitting in the doctor's office, watching my daughter bravely get two shots of Novocain in the head preceding eleven stitches. My husband, who had walked around outside with our son while I was inside holding our daughter's hand as she screamed in pain, said to me when we returned home, "I need a drink." *Who is it that needs a drink?* I thought in disbelief.

Ironically, the little girl who rides a bike, ice skates, skis, and roller blades split open her head running inside with both her parents nearby for supervision.

Stranded in Medical Woes

Isolation and economics are constant problems for mothers at home.

—Heidi L. Brennan, co-director of Mothers at Home, as told to Darcie Sanders and Martha M. Bullen, *Staying Home*

The summer from hell continued with my running back and forth to the dentist, trying to heal my ailing tooth. In the end, despite terrific efforts by my dentist, I lost the tooth to a root canal.

I returned home with throbbing pain to two needy children, one who was just recovering from her eleven stitches and the other who was awake most of the day and night with dental pain of his own; his first teeth were arriving.

Alone in this agony, I wanted to tell my dentist, who is also a mother of two young children—an excellent mother too, I might add—that her job is definitely easier than mine. In fact, I wanted to tell all professional women that their ability to be intellectually challenged and hopefully fulfilled on a regular basis is a breeze compared to the daily grind of caring for young children without any time off, not even for a lunch break on most days.

Choosing to be home for my children is a sacrifice. I don't do this job easily, although I do it consciously, knowing being home for my children during their first five years is in sync with my value system.

I have a lot of hard days, particularly if one or all of us are sick. I'd kill for an hour of downtime, alone, to regroup. Instead, I end up staying sick longer because I have no time to rest. Or there are days when I have a doctor's appointment and the only way I can get there is to take my two children with me, which I have done. Try taking an

66

EKG test while watching your infant crawl over the wires. I cannot believe my heart rate reading was too accurate on that day.

Being a baby boomer caught in the crunch of childcare and eldercare issues, I have a lot of anger about our lack of familial support, too. One day, exhausted from all my caretaking responsibilities, I told my elderly father that it's hard not having anyone to relieve me or my husband. He responded, "Just think, you can say you did it yourself."

The rage I experience every time I feel stranded in this difficult job on a good day sends me to the health club to sanely vent the anger. On a bad day, I resent my husband, furious that his life has not changed as dramatically as mine.

Many at-home mothers, I suspect, cannot even admit to the rage, for to be "good mothers" we must present a happy face, yet statistics show that women at home with children under the age of five have one of the highest rates of depression. Perhaps it's time to acknowledge that emotionally supporting at-home mothers is as crucial to a healthy family as a breadwinner's salary.

No one should do this job alone. You can't continually "give" without some replenishment. Every mother should be able to call in a pitch hitter now and then.

MOTHERING TIPS

Remember—you don't have to be perfect, just loving.

- Take a parenting class. We model what we learn, and since none of us had perfect parents, acquiring new skills can be helpful to your child's upbringing.

- Bathe your young children before supper to relax them during that difficult 4 to 6 p.m. timeframe, also called the "hell hours" by some mothers I know.

- Avoid labeling your child (or letting anyone else do it either) in any way. I remember when my daughter was three years old and everyone kept saying, "She's so shy." I responded, "And she is very kind, too." My daughter is now one of the first to stand up in front of her class and has become a leader.

- End each day asking your children, "What was the best part of your day?" Also, ask them to tell you what they are grateful for. These questions help create more positive, optimistic children.

- Have your babysitter come at least an hour earlier than an event you and your husband are scheduled to attend to give yourselves time alone before socializing with others.

- Don't pressure yourself to have play dates for young toddlers. Most children are not developmentally ready to share at age two. The children will get plenty of socialization when they enter preschool.

- Delegate. A spouse or babysitter can do things from bathing and feeding a child to filling out all those school and camp forms. Even an older child can read a bedtime story to the younger sibling occasionally.

- Do activities with your children—free concerts in the park, ice-skating, nature walks—that you and your spouse enjoy, too. Your life does not have to be child-centered all the time.

- Find humor in the challenges, gifts in the stressful moments. When my daughter got eleven stitches in her head and could not swim in our pool for a week, we took family trips beyond our backyard and rediscovered the area in which we live.

- Accept your children as they are, not for what you wanted to be or want them to be.

- Read *Busy But Balanced: Practical and Inspirational Ways to Create a Calmer, Closer Family* by Mimi Doe, *The Mommy Guide* by Susan Bernard, and *Mothering the New Mother* by Sally Placksin.

A Tender Day

Yet, when we begin to make available to ourselves our own possibilities, it is like drilling a well to an untapped energy reserve, like finding a bank account we haven't yet used. It's the cheapest form of entertainment there is.

—Mildred Newman and Bernard Berkowitz,
How to Be Your Own Best Friend

I awoke on the morning of my fortieth birthday, greeted by my fair-haired, ten-month-old son who tumbled around the bed with me, crawling and falling, then snuggling into my chest. A perfect birthday greeting, orchestrated by my husband, who knew that despite the 6 a.m. hour, that I would be deeply touched by the love of our spunky little infant.

A few hours later, when I joined the family downstairs, red, white, and blue balloons with a similarly colored birthday sign awaited my arrival. My other towhead, my four-and-a-half-year-old precocious daughter, gleefully yelled, "Surprise!" as happy about my birthday as her own. The joys children so innocently and frequently express bring life into perspective so often. I needed her joy today to remind me of my own. Just last night, and the few nights before, I cried about the loss of my youth, the difficult childhood I endured, the friends who chose not to share their journeys with me, and love I didn't get but now know I deserve.

I needed to celebrate all that I have, and I needed to celebrate it quietly, with my family. At my daughter's suggestion, we ate a hearty country breakfast at one of my favorite local eateries, Chipper's Cafe in Ipswich. Years earlier, I wheeled and dealed at

69

Chipper's, meeting the prospective buyer of my lucrative PR business there for the first time. Months later, I was there again, meeting a lawyer to unravel a deal that went sour.

At forty, happily embraced by my family, I preferred to have a high chair with pancakes squished beneath it to the challenges of a fast-track career. That's not to say I didn't think a career was valuable. It was, to me, but only if it worked around my family, not competed with it. My career had been off track for more than five years. At forty, I began getting it back on-track, but at a slower, more balanced pace.

I'm fortunate to be a writer, especially when I give myself permission to write. No one else is going to give it to me. Returning to this book on my fortieth birthday was a commitment to myself— more important than my commitment to lose forty pounds by my fortieth (which I did!).

Other simple pleasures of that day reminded me of what I was going to need during this new decade of my life. Fun began to become a priority. That day, after breakfast, we shopped at a charming toy store for a birthday present for my daughter's friend. I could have stayed in that store all day, playing with the toys, delighting in my daughter's excitement, and hearing my son giggle as my husband wiggled a hand puppet in his face.

On that day I chose to do what made my heart sing—*write!* Being alone in my office in the late afternoon while my husband took our children on errands was to me a perfect treat. I loved the intimacy of writing more than being in a roomful of people. I asked my husband not to give me a party for my fortieth. Between bridal showers, our wedding, and baby showers, I felt others had done enough celebrating with me. At that turning point of my life I just wanted time alone.

I gave myself a party, the type of party an introverted and creative soul like mine cherishes. I worked out for an hour. Exercise is as important to me and my creative process as is solitude. I took a shower and lounged around in a towel before putting on my most comfortable outfit—a fleece top and matching mini skirt. No makeup that day, either. Just comfort. I didn't even want to go out to dinner as my husband suggested. Instead, I opted for a light meal with our children on our rotted-out deck overlooking the pool and indulged in just "being."

I remember thinking, *Tomorrow I will celebrate first-class with my husband alone at an inn of his choice. Next week I will celebrate again with a dear friend who supported me through nearly all of my adult changes.*

But that day was mine. And who I am is a person who appreciates from the bottom of her heart the simple pleasures of time, quality friends, my nuclear family, and a cozy home environment.

Although I spent that summer grieving the losses a new decade of life forces us to encounter, I felt happy. I was happy about the life I was beginning to create and relieved to leave behind decades of stress and struggle. At forty, I knew I had limits, but I also had carefully created beliefs that would take me to my dreams.

On my thirtieth birthday, following a surprise party my friend Bess had arranged on a private sailboat on Boston Harbor, I had to prepare for a trip to New York. I was taking one of my clients on a press tour. I was devastatingly sad to be working alone in a job I couldn't stand instead of home with a husband and family which I craved. I cried all day.

As my new decade began, I felt committed to finishing my book, to supporting my husband in a new business, to sending my beautiful daughter off to kindergarten, and to be planning fall activities with my baby boy.

While I felt a bit withered from the challenges of living forty years, I was invigorated by the tenderness I found within myself to be the person I am—simply complex.

Better and Better

A good parent works him or herself out of a job.

—Penelope Leach, pediatrician

These are some of the things I wish somebody had told me when I was a younger mother:

1. You do come up for air after the first three months of mothering an infant. Those long exhausting days of little sleep end and life forms a routine.

2. Mothers typically endure a greater deal of and more frequent change in lifestyle than fathers, which can cause some additional friction between spouses. If you doubt this assertion, ask: Who usually cancels plans or work to stay home with a sick child?

3. Motherhood is a continual state of transition. Each stage our child encounters also brings you to another level of being. Use the cycles of change for personal growth. For example, when your child needs you less—as he or she enters preschool or elementary grades—do something for yourself. Take a class, plant a garden, learn a new skill, or find a job you like. The older your children become, the more important it is to continually reclaim yourself. Getting lost in your children's lives serves no one. Model the healthy self-care and independence you are trying to teach them. Children admire mothers who pursue a passion or interest outside of parenting; it makes them proud and helps set them free to express their best selves, too.

4. Know that the feelings of isolation, frustration, and self-doubt are universal. You are not a bad mother because you sometimes feel

overwhelmed, burned out, or even angry. The rage some women feel is about the conditions in which they mother—not the role itself. Our society does not support mothers. We ask women to do the most demanding job there is—to parent the next generation of human beings—and we give them no pay or recognition.

5. Trust your instincts. You, more than anybody else, know your child.

6. Lighten up. Mothers are only one influence on a child's life. Fathers, teachers, friends, coaches, and other relations affect a child's well-being, too. The children themselves are each born with a unique purpose. You are only a guide for them. Don't control them; let them find their way in the world.

7. The relationship with your spouse should be your number one priority. As Dr. Phil McGraw, a relationship expert, frequently says, "Children join *your* lives, not the other way around."

8. Mothering gets better and better as you become more confident in the role and as the children evolve into unique human beings. The time involved in total, round-the-clock caretaking of infants and toddlers becomes freed up as the children mature. During the children's first five years, it's sometimes difficult to know that you will experience some level of freedom again.

9. To some mothers, particularly those who stay home full-time with young children, that new sense of freedom can be frightening and overwhelming. "Who am I without my children?" is a question they must ponder. Finding that answer can lead to untapped or long-lost passions. The search can be challenging, but worth every moment of angst. We all have a purpose for living. For some, it is to be full-time mothers. For others, being a mother is a part of their whole purpose. It's OK to want more; the trick for all mothers is knowing how to balance it.

10. Find a way to get some of your own money, even if it is just "pocket money." Using your own resources to make purchases contributes to your sense of worth and helps you feel less dependent on your spouse. Dependency can make you vulnerable.

11. The paybacks for all the self-sacrifice are enormous. My mild-mannered five-year-old son, the one who loved trucks more than anything, now tells me he wants to marry me when he grows up. "I wish you weren't already married to Daddy," he says. My once shy and clingy three-year-old daughter, at age nine, ran for student council and won. I am in awe of her confidence. More impor-

tantly, I am most proud of how happy she tells me she is: "Life just keeps getting better and better, Mom."

Soar

There are two things you give your children. One is roots. The other is wings.

—Anonymous

Dear Catie:

I am no different than most mothers preparing a child for kindergarten. I pray that every bus driver, teacher, school nurse, cafeteria worker, librarian, and volunteer will love and protect you as much as I have.

Yet, I know in order for you to spread your very strong and capable wings, no one should love you as intensely as I have. There has to be a letting go, a physical distance, so you can grow in the way God meant for each and every human being to find his or her unique purpose on Earth.

Intuitively, you've known this. Just two summers ago we napped, wrapped like spoons nestled on our family room loveseat. Last week we snuck in a rare afternoon snooze on my and Daddy's king-size bed, with you on one side and me on the other.

The increasing space between us is healthy, Catie. Those precious, endearing moments of early dependency—when you suckled my breast, clutched my hand, or fell asleep with your chin resting on my shoulder—have prepared you to launch your own soul. You are venturing forth with a foundation of security.

I'll still always try to snatch as much affection as I can from you, but my role as a parent is to help you become independent, and I've taken a lot of cues from you. I honored your wish for privacy a few weeks ago when you and your best friend, Emily, were happily playing. "Don't come in, Mom, please," you said as I was about to check the toy room disaster. The little girl who used to beg for me to stay by her side was now asking me to stay away, which was a huge growth spurt. I'm not so sure that when you're a teenager I'll be as willing to walk away when you ask me.

* * *

I want to say that it seemed like only yesterday when I started your baby book nearly five years ago, and wondered how I'd ever track all the steps from infancy and preschool to your first day of kindergarten. That's a half truth. Our journey together has raced by. But there were many long, exhausting pauses, too, like the winter of double ear-infections, fourteen-hour days of battling a strong-willed two-year-old, rainy indoor weeks, and hectic summers, running from playground to playground.

On one of those fretful days at the playground, when I looked like the haggard mom that I was, a grandmotherly type of woman gently said to me, "Enjoy her now. You only have her to yourself for the first five years."

I couldn't comprehend then, when you were about two-and-a-half years old, that you would grow into the courageous little girl you've become this summer, jumping off the diving board like a frog wearing a facemask, beaming with delight at your own swimming progress.

And now, as I begin the final entry into your baby book, I know you are ready to soar. Despite the current trend of holding back children who were born in the latter half of the year, I listened to my gut, which said to move you forward, even though you have an October birthday. "I want my daughter to be a leader, not a follower," one mother told me of her decision to hold back her summer-born daughter. I want you to be happy Catie, whatever your nature is.

You've shown me in a zillion ways that you're ready to start kindergarten next week, from insisting last spring on walking into your preschool classroom alone, making your bed every morning, bringing in the mail, feeding your baby brother, and writing notes to friends.

So on you go, with my blessing that your kind and nurturing soul finds gentle guidance, warm and true friends, joy in learning, and creative room to unfold.

And I send you with an adult lesson I wish I had learned in kindergarten instead of thirty-five years later following lots of angst.

Follow your heart. Joy is not found in winning others' approval—not even mine; it is untapped by discovering and bringing forward your best self.

If you take the time to be quiet in your busy days of play and learning, you will learn to hear your own voice.

Know this, too: No matter what is going on in your life—from making a new friend to performing a task you're unsure of—you always have a safe place within to go for comfort and guidance. That inner sanctuary connects you to God.

You are not alone. There are angels everywhere. I hope your teacher is one of them.

Guilt

There is no such thing as a well-adjusted slave.

—Wayne W. Dyer, *Pulling Your Own Strings*

I don't know one mother who doesn't feel guilty about the times she thinks she has failed her child, either by forgetting or not being able to attend a youngster's important activity.

Three months before my daughter's elementary school scheduled its fall concert, I had planned a weekend getaway with a good friend. When my daughter cried at my not being able to see her perform, I gave in. I returned early from my weekend to watch the show, forfeiting an entire day with a friend I see only once a year.

Looking back, I made the wrong choice—out of guilt. I resented sitting in the audience that day, especially because my husband and son were also there supporting my daughter. If I had stayed with my friend, my daughter would not have been alone.

Up until that concert, I had been to every one of my daughter's activities for seven years, even if it meant dropping a writing project in midsentence or postponing the start date of a workshop I teach to accommodate her.

A few years later, when confronted with the same dilemma, I made a different choice. I was scheduled to host the first meeting of my new book group, which I started with a neighbor. We had planned the meeting a month earlier, confirming with all the members the time and the place. A week before the book group was to meet, my daughter came home with her basketball schedule. Her very first basketball game ever was scheduled on the same night as my book group.

I told my daughter that her father and brother would attend the first game, but that I would go to her future games. She continued to sulk as I explained that I had committed to several other people not only to attend, but to host my book group. I wanted to model to my daughter that I had a life outside of hers, that I wasn't put on this Earth solely to please her.

That evening when she returned from the game and my book group was still meeting, she raced to her bedroom, glowing about the fact that she scored a basket. My lack of presence didn't make a difference. The next morning both she and my son said at breakfast that they didn't sleep too well that night. "What do you talk about at book group?" my daughter asked. "You were all laughing so hard." My son thought it was silly that his preschool teachers, Mrs. Higgins and Mrs. Mahoney, who are members of my book group, could have so much fun outside of school.

In choosing for that one night and other occasions thereafter to fulfill myself, I gave both my children a valuable lesson: Mothers are people with needs, too. And when we fulfill those needs, we become more fun and loving mothers.

Gratitude

When we write down or acknowledge in some way the gifts in our lives, we can't help but feel good—we put our attention on the bounty in our days rather than the lack.

—Mimi Doe with Marsh Walch, *10 Principles of Spiritual Parenting*

There are some days when I miss my daughter very much. One day in particular I found myself looking at her black suede shoes, which were stashed by the fireplace; I longed to hold her, to tell her what a beautiful child she is. Instead, because she was in school, I sat and allowed my heart to fill up with all the love I have for her. Tears of joy streamed down my face.

Later that day, lucky enough to sneak a brief afternoon nap, I laid down in my daughter's antique canopy bed. Again, my heart filled up with love as I glanced around her happy (and cluttered) room. My daughter had become such a wonderful young lady and a friend.

During the infant, toddler, and preschool years, when I was doing all the caregiving, I couldn't even envision the payback I would feel for the constant nurturing I provided. And the payback is huge. On days when I came home from working at my husband's new bakery, with an aching back from bending over the bread case all day long, she would give me a massage. On hectic mornings when I had to get two kids ready for school by myself because my husband left to bake at 2:30 a.m., my daughter would help me prepare my son's breakfast.

While her help is always greatly appreciated, it was her emerging spirit that touched my soul. She tells me at least two or three

80

times a day how much she loves me. At night, just before she goes to bed, she often snuggles in my and my husband's king-size bed with me alone, and we become "the bookworms"—reading and laughing together. Together, we've skated, cross-country skied, studied falling snowflakes, cooked, danced, and swum.

We've become our own little team, each of us growing in different ways. I've learned so much from my daughter. One day, when she was skipping around the house as she so often does, I asked her if seven is a happy age. "Yes, Mom. At seven, you have nothing to worry about except your friends. You don't have to worry about a business or making money."

The next morning, when I watched her walk down our driveway to meet the school bus, she was observing each of her boots as they touched the newly fallen snow. She was so fully in the present—so content. I vowed to focus on the present for longer moments myself.

Another fun part of watching her evolve was the unpredictably of her behavior. She can be the sweetest, kindest little girl one moment—gently stroking "Truffles," her guinea pig—and then a cool, mini-teenager the next—swinging her hips and singing to the beats of Justin Timberlake. Each time she sways to the older side, I am reminded that my time with her is so short. I want to cherish every moment.

June Cleaver

What if you were told that your life was a sacred prayer your child took as the formula for a spiritual presence? When we acknowledge ourselves first and foremost as spiritual beings we can't help but shift our parenting energy into a higher place. Exploring our own sacred selves enhances our connection with our kids.

—Mimi Doe, *Busy But Balanced*

I don't bake the perfect brownies, drive my kids to endless activities, talk calmly to them all the time as I discipline—even though I once tried to be June Cleaver, a superficial image of the ideal mother.

I also tried briefly to emulate some of the well-groomed, picture-perfect-looking moms I know. That's not me. I'm a writer, who needs to leave her house messy when she finds the sentence she spent all night looking for and rushes to the computer instead. Some days, if I'm in a creative flow, I don't even get out of my pajamas until 4 p.m.

Although my image differs from the perfect TV mom, I am an excellent mother in my own way. The gift I give my children is working through my pain so I don't impose it on them. I am truthful and authentic.

They've seen me cry when I was sad, yell (more often than I would have liked) when I'm mad, laugh when I'm silly, rest when I'm tired. They've seen me at work and at play, up and down. I've modeled both frustration and success. I've modeled dispute and moving through conflict. I've shown them my humanness, which is imperfect.

I also see their souls and know when they need downtime, hugs, and simply my presence. Through the winter months we've spent more time inside the house connecting than outside. These hibernation periods let us get to know one another more intimately than the frantic, overscheduled lives our society encourages, even of our littlest ones. Instead of a rush to get somewhere, we revel in being, not going.

June Cleaver "looked good." I'm focusing my children and myself on "feeling" good as whole, centered, and loving people.

THOUGHTS ON PROTECTING YOUR SELF-ESTEEM

Don't lose yourself in mothering.

- Stay visible. Get out of isolation. Take an adult education class, pursue a hobby, start a book group, join a team, or run for office at your local library or parent-teachers associations.

- Keep connected with your women friends. Your spouse cannot fulfill all of your emotional needs as a new mother.

- Choose friends based on mutual interests and values, not simply according to the age of your children. Count your blessings if you find a friend with similar values who also has children the same age as yours.

- Plan a mother's retreat at least once a year, either alone or with a friend, so you stay connected to who you are besides a caregiver.

- Meditate, exercise, and create moments of solitude as frequently as possible to keep yourself centered.

- Visit the Internet website www.esteemedwoman.com.

- Read *Self and Soul: A Woman's Guide to Enhancing Self-Esteem through Spirituality* by Adele Wilcox and *The Woman's Comfort Book: A Self-Nurturing Guide for Restoring Balance in Your Life* by Jennifer Louden.

Letting Go

There are only two things in the entire world that are within your control: 1. The way you choose to feel about yourself. 2. Your behaviors, which are based on your feelings ... As long as we foster an illusion of control and feel responsible for things which are out of our control, we cannot live the reality of our lives and we cannot gain a mastery of ourselves.

—Susanna McMahon, *The Portable Therapist*

Motherhood is a continual state of letting go, loosening the reins, and surrendering.

At first, women who become mothers must let go of many of their own needs (especially sleep) in order to nurture an infant twenty-four hours a day. Then, as our babies grow into preschoolers and kindergartners, we begin to let our children fend for themselves more. "Work it out," we tell two squabbling young friends or siblings. "You can do it," we say as we encourage the little ones to try a new skill.

It's when our children start asserting their desire for less of us that we really need to listen to and honor them, even when it hurts. My five-year old, in mimicking his older sister who now gets changed behind closed doors, won't even let me see him naked anymore, even though I once changed his diapers. I need to finally let go of my baby and accept that he is a little boy with a mind of his own.

My daughter, who up until age nine loved every minute she spent with me, began to prefer hanging out with her father, which is a usual development at her age, according to *Your Nine-Year-Old Child* by Louise Bates Ames and Carol Chase Haber. This book is one in a series produced from The Gesell Institute of Human Development, which also offers excellent overviews of children ages one through fourteen. Fathers, in fact, play an increasingly important role in the self-esteem of girls age eleven and beyond, many research studies show.

"One of the major changes that takes place at nine years of age is that the child gradually detaches himself from his mother. At eight he hung on her every word, absorbed her attention, wanted her constant company," the authors claim. "This is a time for a mother to step back, draw a sigh of relief, appreciate her new freedom, and be glad that her child is growing out of the dependence and entanglement with her that actually she may have found trying a few short months earlier. The child's newfound independence can actually be a big plus all around."

When I stepped back and observed my newly independent young daughter, I was sad to realize she is already past the halfway mark of her life with me. In eight years, it is likely that she will be off to college. Where did the time go? And just when she grew so much more interesting as a person because of her intellectual development, she needs her friends more than me. It doesn't seem fair that through all the terrible twos when mothers would leap at the chance to have a few minutes relief, we get none. Then, at age nine when the child is so much fun, we get less of her.

A friend with teenage children warns me that I haven't even begun the letting go process. "You definitely lose them during the adolescence. The teenagers will tell you that you are clueless about their lives, and you know what? You are," she says. "Teenagers also teach you that perfection is an illusion. No matter how well you have parented up to this point, you learn there are many factors beyond your control. You can't pick their friends, choose their study habits, or be with them as they drive away."

Two friends of mine are struggling with loss of control with children who are much younger. One friend gave birth to a child with cerebral palsy. Up until that point, she lived the ideal image of "the perfect family." Her husband is a lawyer, they live in an affluent community by the sea, and they have two other beautiful children, a boy and a girl, and part-time help that gave my friend freedom to explore her independent interests. Her third child's diagnosis changed all that. Her days are now filled with doctors' and physical therapy appointments and teaching her child how to walk with a crutch.

ADVICE ON MOVING BEYOND MOTHERHOOD

Extending ourselves is how we grow.

• Accept that you are entitled to find self-expression outside of your family's needs.

• Trust that the skills you developed in mothering are transferable. After all, being a mother is like running a business. You've already proven you're an entrepreneur.

• Despite media images to the contrary, many women who choose to return to work after being home with children prefer part-time, flexible employment over the fast-track jobs they had before kids. For this reason, women are starting new businesses in record numbers.

• Pay well those who support you in quality childcare. As you know firsthand, caring for children is valuable work.

• Acknowledge tradeoffs and dismiss the Superwoman myth. Remember the army's slogan: "Be all you can be." A suggestion I read somewhere said to replace that with "Be all you want to be." Let go of the perfectly clean house when you add a new job or passion to your life.

Another friend, as perfect a mother as one can strive to be, learned that her bright eight-year old has obsessive-compulsive disorder, which is a brain abnormality. No matter how hard my friend tried to be the mother who always fed her child nutritional meals, kept her daughter in stimulating activities, and stayed home with the hopes of providing more security for her youngster, she could not prevent a medical condition.

Working harder at mothering or accepting all the responsibility for our children is not the answer. For example, even in disciplining children, we do not need to be overly involved, according to pediatrician Sanford Matthews, author of *Through the Motherhood Maze.* Matthews says that when mothers come to him, distraught because the disciplining of their children is going badly, he advises these mothers to concentrate on making their own lives more rewarding rather than merely emphasizing their relationship with their children.

These little beings that bless our lives have fates of their own. We can drive ourselves crazy trying to mold them into perfection, but like us adults, they have their own journeys. We can only guide them. Then we have to trust that our children will master the same task which we adults continually work on: finding their own way through the obstacle course of life without too many bruises.

III. PARENTING THE PARENTS

Introduction

If we are to successfully manage the care of our parents, we have to learn, first of all, to care for ourselves.

—Claire Berman,
Caring for Yourself While Caring for Your Aging Parents

If you are a baby boomer, the chances are high that one day you will be thrust into the role of caregiver for one or both of your parents—a role for which you have been given no preparation. Handling the maze of misinformation, incompetent bureaucratic systems, and the lack of "care" in our health services industry are just a few of the challenges that may lead you to feel the greatest stress of your life.

Here is the reality: In 1994 there were 33 million Americans over the age of sixty-five. According to the U.S. Census Bureau, that number is expected to double—to about 75 million—over the next forty years. The population of people eighty-five and older will triple to more than 11 million, according to Claire Berman, in *Caring for Yourself While Caring for Your Aging Parents*. Most importantly, she notes, "People are not just living longer; they are living longer with disability."

Two-thirds of all Americans are involved in looking after someone—a family member, an older friend, or a neighbor—according to *The Caregiver's Sourcebook*. The majority of caregivers are married women between the ages of forty and sixty-five, according to Boomers International, an Internet Web site.

I have listened to my best friend, a mother of a three-year-old and an eight-year-old, juggle the needs of her young family with the multitude of caretaking requirements for her eighty-nine-year-old father. She has been doing double duty, including managing her father's three-tenant apartment building, for several years. She begins her jammed-packed days of caregiving by awakening an hour earlier than her family to sit alone with a cup of coffee. That is her only break of the day. I ask her how she manages, and she tells me about her own declining health. "I have cataracts in my eyes, and I'm only forty-four years old."

My own care-giving responsibilities have complicated any attempts to plan a fun retreat. Between February and December 2001, my parents were taken by ambulance to either a hospital, nursing home, or eventually to their assisted-living facility ten times! Each trip cost us $230 beyond what their individual health insurers covered.

The chronic stress of that year began with a call from my brother, telling me that my father had suffered a stroke. My brother found him incoherent, pale, and foaming at the mouth one morning when he casually dropped by to say hello. The stroke turned out to be a TIA, which is a milder neurological malfunction that left him temporarily paralyzed on the left side of his face.

My father was released a few days later, much to our shock. My brother and I had hoped he would be hospitalized a lot longer. I was never sure if it was a medical decision or an insurance dictate that sent him home earlier than appeared wise. Two days later, he collapsed on the bathroom floor. Fortunately, I was talking to my mother on the phone at the time, and I called 911.

It was clear to my brother and me at this point that my parents should no longer be living alone. Convincing my parents of the need to move to a safer environment was a different story. My father, a construction supervisor who had retired just three months earlier at age seventy-eight, could not accept the rapid decline of his frail body. He met our concerns for him with anger and denial.

I ended up researching for a geriatric case manager to help us. We hired a firm comprised of social workers, one of whom had much experience in dealing with mentally ill persons like my mother. Their wisdom and assistance helped through a few crises. Still, managing our parents' health care needs was a full-time job for both my brother and me.

We tried to split the tasks, but the sibling who lives closer tends to take on more of the work. This unfairness causes even more stress than taking care of your parents, according to Berman. In her book, she quotes a study by sociologists J. Suitor and Karl Pillemer: "Reports by caregivers indicated ... that siblings were overwhelmingly the most important source of interpersonal stress."

My brother lived closer, so he did most of the day-to-day work, including running to each hospital and nursing home to fill out all the paperwork. Yet on the days when I visited my parents, I sometimes spent two hours battling Boston commuter traffic. I could have traveled to another state in the time it took me to reach my parents.

I spent four to six hours a day on the phone, trying to get answers to medical questions, changing health care policies, and finding an attorney who specialized in eldercare. Regrettably, my son, three years old at the time, spent too much time in front of a TV set.

Through the many tense and frantic moments, my brother repeatedly pointed out that our parents never had to go through for their parents what we were going through. "It gets to the point where you don't even want to answer the phone anymore. There is always a problem," my brother remarked.

Later, when I asked my brother for any insights he had on elderly caretaking, he said, "There should be a course on how to set up your life. The end of your life is just as important as the beginning, yet there's no training for that stage, as there is when you're preparing for college or something."

In the following section I highlight some of my intense care-giving moments, with the hope that readers embarking upon a similar journey may find companionship and insight.

Double Whammy

Your state of mind is your responsibility. Whether we experience peace or conflict is determined by the choice we make in how we see people and situations, whether we see them worthy of love or as justifying our fear. We do not have to act like robots and give others the power to determine whether we will experience love or fear, happiness or sadness.

—Gerald G. Jampolsky, *Love Is Letting Go Of Fear*

One day my father had a mini-stroke. My mother already had a heart ailment and signs of colon cancer. In addition to their illnesses, they were elderly and isolated. My brother and I—especially my brother—helped a great deal.

That we had two aging parents to care for, both with physical problems and one with mental problems, was overwhelming, considering that I also had two young children and a business to run. I'd been praying and meditating for relief.

Alone in the chaos, I made a choice I've learned to make several times when I've made a conscious effort to heal. I could give in to the fear that I couldn't handle the situation and remain paralyzed in fright. Or, I could decide I had the resources to manage all the stress around me.

In choosing the latter strategy, I opted to sit quietly in a chair and remember this thought: *I am not alone.* Then, I followed up with another thought: *I am safe and supported.* My fright then subsided.

Later that same day a babysitter called to say she could come Saturday when I had to meet with another advisor regarding my parents' situation. After that, my father's sister called to check in. My cousin, who is a doctor, called to explain in layman's terms the body's reaction during a stroke and the subsequent care needed. My husband offered to stay home from work to help out. When my father's social workers failed to address my mother's fragile emotional state, I pursued my mother's psychiatrist, who returned my calls within hours. He arranged for me to speak with a hospital liaison. "I can hear the stress in your voice," she calmly reassured me as I tried to explain the situation with my three- and seven-year old screaming in the background. With empathy and confidence, she assured me a psychiatric nurse would visit my mother the next day, the same day my father would be being released from the hospital.

After lying awake all that night, I came to another realization. I didn't need a nurse to visit my mother on the same day as my father's return home. Assessing two conditions simultaneously seemed confusing and would only add to the stress, instead of reduce it. I called back and asked to reschedule my mother's nurse's visit for next week.

I was too exhausted to handle both my parents' situations in the same morning. I would evaluate the situation more clearly with some distance between the two events.

In the past, I'd handled it all alone, often reacting quickly, rather than pondering options. So have my parents. This time, knowing my health was equally important, I didn't. I reached out. And I also set the pace at which I could most effectively think clearly.

I still felt enormous sadness at my parents' deteriorating health and was exhausted from the physical demands of visiting my parents ninety minutes away and being home for my family, too. But I knew I could handle it. I was making smart decisions.

Authority/Trust

"Authority," as defined in the MacMillan Dictionary for Children:

1. The power or right to make decisions, command, act or control: The captain has authority over the sailors on a ship. *2. A person or group having this power or right:* We reported the car accident to the authorities. *3. A good source of information or facts:* That professor is an authority on the life of Abraham Lincoln.

"I'm letting you and your brother handle everything," my father told me the night he was released from the hospital. As the days progressed, it became clear that my father was allowing my brother to be his taxi driver, errand boy, and grocery shopper. He was letting me make calls to relatives, social workers, nurses, and even the Milton police when he fell on the bathroom floor after arriving home from the hospital.

But he was not allowing either of us to manage his financial or long-term health requirements. All the research my brother and I did to protect both of my parents was ignored. Trying to help someone who won't listen is infuriating, and my brother and I both had the stomach aches to prove it. More hurtful, though, was that my father wanted to hand over the responsibility for his life choices to us (as he did through much of my youth, leaving me alone with my hysterical mother while he went away for the weekend). Yet he refused to give us the authority to manage the responsibility. We had no access to his funds to provide my parents with services to support them. We were not allowed to make any decisions that may have been in the best interest of my parents. Most hurtful of all was the repeat of our old childhood story—we were not supposed to have any needs. My father refused to hear that I couldn't take him to a doctor's appointment because I needed to pick up my three-year old from preschool and wait for my seven-year old to get off the school bus two and half hours later. He called one night, asking me to drive the three-hour roundtrip to his house to buy him a birthday card for a relative. My brother, who also had two young children and a stressful project management job, was exhausted from running to my parents' house to their numerous doctor appointments and then returning to his own family, whom he loves very much. My father showed no concern for the health of his children.

Saddest of all was that my father had the resources to get outside help. He refused to use them.

In trying to see this tragic, seemingly never-ending story from my father's perspective, I felt enormous compassion for a seventy-nine-year-old man who could no longer drive—a major freedom had been removed from his life. Yet I knew his driving was a safety threat to others. My father's ailing legs were not able to touch the brake in time to save his or another's life.

That he became dependent on others when he didn't know how to ask for help from resources available to him was sad. He trusted no one, not even his own son and daughter, though we'd been there for him our entire lives.

He lived in denial, telling my brother everything would be fine when things returned to normal (he's been telling us that story for nearly thirty years). The problem is, as my brother tried desperately to explain, that things would never return to normal now.

My parents had major health issues that needed to be addressed. In addition to my father's stroke, he also had prostate cancer, asbestosis from working in the Quincy Shipyard, diabetes, and blocked arteries in his leg that caused him to collapse as frequently as three times a week. In addition to his woes, my mother's fragile psychological condition was always a concern.

My brother generously offered them a comfortable living space in one of his nearby apartments. They declined.

They continued to struggle on alone, irresponsibly refusing help, and we didn't have the authority to change that—only they did.

I wanted my dad to know I was there for him. He had a choice, and no one would remove that freedom from him, but he couldn't delegate it to me either. His life was his responsibility.

Going to the Wall

Burnout, however, signals not despair, but hope. Recognized and attended to, it can become a positive energy force, signifying the time has come for a cease-and-desist action, a hard look at yourself, and a chance to do something new.

—Herbert Freudenbuerger,
Burnout: How to Beat the High Cost of Success

My father called me one day, two hours before he was scheduled for a doctor's visit he had forgotten about. "I need you to give me a ride. Your brother can't take me," he directed me.

He made a huge step forward in first asking the local Elder Services' van to take him to his visit. The office declined, giving my brother, my father, and me three different reasons for refusal.

I couldn't possibly make it to his house, ninety minutes away, in time to get him to his appointment. Besides, I had a seven-year old getting off a school bus in a few hours. "Dad, you need to call a taxi," I told him. Angrily, he hung up, telling me he'd figure out a solution.

A few hours later, my brother called to tell me my father had taken a taxi to his appointment. He had told my brother he'd rather have paid him the fifty dollars than the cab driver. My brother didn't want the money; he wanted the time to attend to his very stressful project management job. He'd been transporting both my father and mother for the past fourteen days while trying to keep a job and family intact.

I was sad that I couldn't be physically present for my father all the times he needed me. He forced me, on many occasions, to choose

94

between my parents' needs and my children's needs, leaving me agonizing over priorities.

When I was younger I did as I was told, no matter the cost to my own emotional well-being. "Be there. She's your mother," he'd tell me on dreadful holidays I spent at home with a mother who, because of memory loss due to shock treatments, could not recall my age (she bought me dolls for Christmas when I was eighteen) or acknowledge my presence. Questions about how I was adjusting to my freshman year at college were never asked. The focus, instead, was on keeping my mother calm and out of a psychiatric ward. Frozen in my emotions, I was afraid to say or do anything that would upset her.

Twenty-four years later, I needed to call some of the shots with my father. My parents will always be my parents, but my children come first now. It's not an easy decision, especially when the manipulative "help me" is uttered.

ADVICE ON CAREGIVING

Mother Theresa was saint-like; you do not have to be.

• Men and women generally handle the tasks of caring for their elderly parents differently. It is important for family members to know and honor their different styles of coping with the stress of caregiving. According to the National Alliance for Caregiving, males often demonstrate a more distanced, hands-off, practical approach, especially to the emotional aspects of caring for a person who is sick or depressed. This approach makes them less vulnerable than women to feeling depressed and overwhelmed. Women tend to get more emotionally involved and visit the sick relative more often.

• Hire competent help: geriatric managers, visiting nurses, and childcare support.

• Pamper yourself every chance you get. Get that massage, go for a walk, read a good book.

• Insist on getting power of attorney for your parent(s).

• Enlist the support of family members and friends; if these people are scarce or emotionally unavailable, join a caregivers' support group or seek professional counseling.

• Say no when you are too exhausted—physically or emotionally—to take on anymore. Your health is important, too.

• Use this time to find a deeper connection with a loved one. Say the things you've held back, ask the questions you want answered, and see the world through the elder's eyes.

I do care. I spent hours on the phone seeking competent support services for my parents, including professionals who can develop long-term health care plans for both of them. Although these are responsibilities my father should have handled and refused to do, I couldn't leave my parents hanging. I chose to support them in my own way.

I used my intelligence to research licensed geriatric care managers (they exist) to provide backup to my parents when they were declined van rides by services designated to supply them. I investigated ways that they could best use their retirement assets to support their current lifestyle. I checked in regularly to let him know I loved them and cared, even when my father infuriated me and refused to acknowledge my needs or concerns about him.

I just couldn't be his sidekick anymore, complying with whatever directive he gave me. I needed to go to the wall and demand that he take some responsibility for his care too.

Sometimes love really is tough.

Advocate

The most painful legacy of having a parent or sibling with mental illness is the feeling of utter helplessness, the sense that no matter what you do nothing will change and no one will listen. The most profound act of courage is to recognize and to engage in the hard work of overcoming that despair.

—Victoria Secunda, *When Madness Comes Home: Help and Hope for the Children, Siblings, and Partners of the Mentally Ill*

My kind uncle—my mother's brother—was calling me regularly to check in about my parents' declining health. After explaining to him that I needed to find a separate social worker for my mother—my father had been assigned his own—he said to me, "You are your mother's advocate now."

His words hit me hard and they echoed throughout my head for days. I was forced into that advocacy role as a teenager, unsure how to get help. Back then, committing my hallucinating mother was one deed. Attending family therapy sessions that focused exclusively on my mother was another. Clarifying my mother's mental state was an ongoing process. Once, she was termed "manic depressive" and given shock treatments that supposedly induced a memory loss of up to three weeks as a side effect. Instead, there were years when she would not even talk, and the silence was as frightening as her previous screams of terror. Eventually, she was diagnosed a schizophrenic and spent years in and out of mental hospitals.

Today my mother, calmed into a nearly catatonic state by drugs powerful enough to free her from a psychiatric ward, has different needs. She lives at home in a filthy, smelly house with my father, sleeping and smoking through her days. Baths, housekeeping, and cooking are foreign to her.

People who are uneducated about mental illness—including some of my own extended family—think incorrectly that being my mother's daughter gives me control over her, but I do not have it. I cannot clean her, dress her, and feed her to make her look presentable in order to save the family from the shame of having a relative who often looks like a bag lady. For many of my adolescent and college years, I tried unsuccessfully to do all of the aforementioned, and more. Many schizophrenics do not care what they look like, smell like, or what they eat. And in their diagnosed apathy, these mentally ill persons could care less what you or I think of them either. Any attempts to help them are often met with distrust or disinterest, both of which are painful. Nonetheless, for a long time I bought into others' beliefs that as a dutiful daughter I could help my mother. I even once thought that with enough love and attention I could possibly cure her.

Now I understand that in my advocacy role I need to teach this: At present, schizophrenia has no known cure. As hurtful as it is to watch a physically healthy-looking person remain as unkempt as a homeless person, no amount of my attention will change the brain signals that tell my mother it is OK not to care. She not only fails to care about herself, she cannot express emotion to those she has loved. When her parents died, my mother did not shed a tear. When I was getting married, she kept asking who would button her dress on my wedding day. When I asked her to hold on to the phone and listen to me after my father collapsed on the bathroom floor, she hung up on me, leaving me no choice but to call 911 for help.

Mental illness affects at least one quarter of American families, many of whom suffer in silence the painful stigma. Even Alzheimer's patients and their families often get care and understanding. A schizophrenic is often met with disbelief, such as how could a perfectly normal person function in filth and nonchalance?

The truth is they are not normal, and we all have to accept that and treat them accordingly.

To treat my seventy-one-year-old mother in her later years, I know now she needs different care than my father. She needs a social worker and/or nurse who understands that my mother is scared to have someone else in the house. She needs doctors in the medical community that know, while my mother should quit smoking, that to many schizophrenics the charge smoking gives them is often their only solace. Cigarettes are to them what chocolate is to some women with PMS. They simply need to have it.

She needs to have others physically care for her, like bringing her food, even though she distrusts them and is totally dependent on my father. If left alone, she will not eat a meal, although she'll devour plenty of candy and other junk food. She needs to be recognized for having some feelings, even though she cannot express them. Once, a few years ago, she told me she prays every night for three things: my brother, me, and that God will take her before my dad.

Her biggest fear, like mine once was, is to be left alone. My advocacy role is to be sure she isn't. My mother will not rot away in a psychiatric ward. I will find her the most suitable setting, using any inheritance, if necessary. My challenge will be to accept that I did the best I could, even though I couldn't cure her or make her look more socially acceptable.

Duped

There will be moments when creating a high-quality life will require you to disappoint others. Bear in mind that there is a spiritual principle that operates in life—when you take good care of yourself, it's in the best interest of the other person as well.

—Cheryl Richardson, *Take Time for Your Life*

I was grumpy, frustrated, and angry, unbearable to live with. I couldn't even stand myself, so I could only imagine how those I lived with felt. I tried to find my private spaces, like soaking in the bathtub for two hours until my prune-like fingers and toes couldn't take it anymore. I screamed tears of rage, alone in my room, before finally collapsing in bed like a wilted rag doll.

Everyone—especially my husband—who acted passive in the least way was on my hit list. I had distanced myself from friends who waited for me to initiate an activity, when they in fact had more time and energy to do so at this point in their lives. Or worse, the friends who had me initiate a task and then became angry at me for not following through in a way they would have liked.

What I needed to say was: NO MORE! Don't look to me to carry you. I can't do it any more. It's self-preservation for me to say NO!

I tried to hand the baton over when I started my first business. I thought I gave my partner the lead, suggesting she be the president and I the vice president. The titles never accurately reflected the responsibilities; eventually we became co-owners and account managers before dissolving the mistake altogether.

A couple years later I tried transferring my PR agency to a woman I wanted to believe was more experienced and excited about the business than I was. Wrong again. We spent five years in court—a painful lesson for me about trusting gut instincts. I felt uneasy about her the first time I met her, but a colleague had told me she was "honorable." Fine-tuning discernment takes practice.

And then I was facing my father, a man I'd spent the majority of my life feeling sorry for. His burdens—caring for a schizophrenic wife—seemed too much for one person to bear. So I took them on for many years, many of my young and innocent years when I should have been learning about life through play and discovery instead of trauma and fear. I became a surrogate spouse to my father, sharing daily in all the pain of dealing with schizophrenia. I even invited my father on some of my dates. He always befriended my boyfriends, sometimes ignoring me in the process. He'd also distance himself from me each time my mother returned home from a hospital stay. No wonder, to this day, when I felt less than the number one priority with my husband, I started feeling a rage brewing within me. I'd been pushed aside a lot.

I thought I dropped some of the responsibility when I married and had my own family, but I didn't really. I made sure my father came on our family vacations to get respite from my mother, ignoring the fact that I, too, needed rest from caring for infants round the clock. I encouraged him to take his yearly solo vacations to Florida to visit with his brother and sister, even though he left my mother without adequate back-up care, sometimes not calling her for days. My brother and I were expected to be there for her, even though she often wouldn't answer the phone and she refused to stay with either one of us.

Each time I read a story about a new drug for schizophrenia, I'd call my father with the news and suggest he ask my mother's psychiatrist about it. More often than not my father chose to "leave well enough alone." He is making that same choice now, refusing to see that he and my mother eventually may need long-term health care and the proper insurance to cover the costs.

His refusal to listen sent me researching high-quality geriatric care managers. Although I'm thrilled to have located an agency to support my parents, I'm furious that my father once again delegated the responsibility to me. I'm angrier still that I took it.

In all my sorrow for my father, I put myself aside. I was no martyr; rather, I was a sensitive soul who desperately wanted to be loved. The problem with that strategy, which I've used throughout most of my adult life, is that working harder doesn't get us love.

Being loving does. And it's hard to be loving if we're angry or exhausted.

I've done the rescue mission many times with my husband and friends, too. I ran myself to exhaustion, helping my husband launch a business and then stay afloat, even though I had two young children depleting my energy on the other end. One childhood friend suffered many tragedies, losing two sisters to diabetes at a young age and growing up fatherless. I let her off the hook a lot for mistreating me, thinking her pain made her less accountable.

The truth is we all have pain, and we are all accountable for handling it. I can't even blame my father for letting me take so much responsibility for my mother's care. That he is passive is infuriating. Just like he had the choice to find alternative, perhaps healthier care for my mother and did not, I have the choice to say NO! I can't handle it anymore for you—especially if you don't listen to and respect me.

I've been duped by myself. Taking on my father's responsibilities as if they were my own nearly killed me. Describing the fatigue I've felt to a therapist friend, I said it felt like there were several twelve-foot granite slabs flattened against my chest. Lifting them seems impossible. "I pray to God to relieve me of these burdens," I cried. My friend responded, "God doesn't lift them. You do. You have the power to remove them."

At first I wanted to blast them away. Now, I see them slowly crumbling to the ground. Each time I try to lift a slab I need to tell myself it's OK not to take on someone's responsibility. I am not selfish. I am exhausted. I need to care for me, too, or I have nothing to give anyone. Self-care will get me through the challenges of aging parents. Yesterday I got my nails and makeup done. Today I cross-country skied in our backyard. I need to replenish or I'm useless. This time it is I who needs compassion. I'm running on empty. I have nothing to give. Can someone else take the reins for a day? By taking the reins, I don't mean caretake. I mean make a decision. Take charge. Initiate. Be responsible. Stand on the frontline; batter up, go to the plate. I need to lay low in the bleachers for a while.

Mom/Role Reversal

Often, in reclaiming the freedom to be who we are, we remember some basic human quality, an unsuspected capacity for love or compassion or some other part of our common birthright as human beings. What we find is almost always a surprise, but it is also familiar—like something we have put in the back of a drawer long ago. Once we see it, we know it as our own.

—Rachel Naomi Remen, *Kitchen Table Wisdom*

My brother and I finally found a beautiful home for my parents in an assisted-living complex, located within miles of where my dad grew up. One day, after returning Dad back to his new apartment following one of his many doctor appointments, I saw my mom sitting alone at a table in the main dining room. I ached for her. Soon, my mother, after forty-seven years of married life, will be eating all her meals alone at that table. My father's prostate cancer has spread to his lymph nodes. He is expected to die within six to twelve months.

I've cried a lot about my Dad's impending death. I was sad for my mother. The only person who had stood by my mother all her life was my father. Yet, as a friend so poignantly noted, the universe works in miraculous ways. Before my father's health declined so dramatically, my mother did nothing for herself. She lay on a sofa, smoking cigarettes all day.

Now my mother is becoming more independent and healthier each day. Smoke-free, she also eats three meals a day instead of candy and chocolate.

CAREGIVER RESOURCES

Suggestions from the National Family Caregivers Association:

• *Share the Care* by Cappy Caposella and Sheila Warnock, a practical and inspirational guide to setting up support groups.

• *The Comfort of Home: An Illustrated Step-by-Step Guide for Caregivers* by Maria Meyer with Paula DerrBeth Writogen McLeod, designed to help untrained caregivers understand what help is needed and where to find resources.

• *Coping With Your Difficult Older Parent: A Guide for Stressed-Out Children* by Grace Lebow.

• *Taking Time for Me: How Caregivers Can Effectively Deal With Stress* by Katherine L. Karr, personal accounts that demonstrate how to renew strength without jeopardizing care.

My brother and I finding new housing and support for both my parents helped them enormously by placing them in a safe and nurturing environment.

But something cosmic happened, too. Roles reversed.

Two weeks after my father moved from a nursing home into his new apartment, about which he was so excited that he counted the days until he arrived, his health deteriorated fast. He went from walking independently with a cane, then a walker, then to being a confined to a wheelchair. He is finally, after a lifetime of caregiving, resting. Tragically, his got his respite in ill health.

It is my mother who now takes care of my father, pushing him about in his wheelchair. It is she, who was silent for many years, who talks to the health care aides.

In all his efforts to protect my mother, my father actually taught her dependence.

Or, from my mother's perspective, by choosing dependence on my dad, she lost herself.

Now that she can no longer depend on him to meet her most basic needs, my mother is thriving on her own. She gets better and better every day, and no one has changed her medicine either.

I've spent my adult life worrying about who would take care of my mother, should something happen to my father. It never crossed my mind, before I started learning self-sufficiency, that my mother would rise to the occasion. After all, she prayed to die before my dad. God apparently had another plan for my mom. She will taste the freedom of personal responsibility.

Like mother, like daughter; we're both writing new stories. *The miracle is not the event—it is the change in the thought that occurs before the event.* My mom inadvertently fulfilled her childhood dream of becoming a teacher. By her example, she taught—even the most disabled of us all—that we are capable of changing a thought that does not serve us well.

We all must stand alone at some point to survive and prosper. My mom is to be admired.

Managed Care

Information is one of the most important coping mechanisms you can have.

—Claire Berman, *Caring for Yourself While Caring for Aging Parents*

Managed care is not managed at all. Ask anyone who is trying to take care of an elderly person. It's more like jumping from minefield to minefield, hoping amidst the chaos and confusion and even fright, that there's a caring—or better yet, a competent person—at the end of the line somewhere.

Try getting through to the appropriate person at a health management organization (HMO). Plan on spending at least thirty minutes surfing through voice mail options, and then hope the person who finally answers has the expertise to provide accurate information.

One day I called and verified my parents' health care policies. The day it was to be in effect, which coincided with the day my father was having an angioplasty on his leg, I learned the policy was never changed correctly. It took my threatening the manager with a call to the media for her to agree to make the necessary changes that her inept employee did not initiate.

My brother, who is managing both of our parents' finances, has on numerous occasions been double billed. Once he received duplicate tax bills on my parents' house. Another time the ambulance company billed him twice for the same service. Twice the insurer initially refused to pay for treatments for which my father qualified. It wasn't until my brother, already strapped for time due to his own hectic project management job and life with two young children, decided to write letters challenging those decisions that reimbursement was finally received. Can you imagine a frail elderly person catching the mistakes my alert brother did?

Then there's the slew of misinformation passed among the several doctors involved in my parents' care. One doctor, a primary care physician, says my father's cancer is stage three; another, the oncologist, says stage four. One doctor says his cancer is under control; another says it spread to the lymph nodes. Then there's a third doctor, a gastroenterologist, who claims that my father could live two more years, even though his liver is more than 90 percent gone. Who do you believe in order to plan the appropriate care?

One doctor agreed to provide hospice services for my father so he would die with dignity and respect. Another wouldn't even acknowledge that my father was dying and scheduled him an appointment, as though it would do him any good. The third doctor requested that my father, who could barely stand, never mind walk, go to the hospital for a set of MRI X-rays that had already been taken earlier in the week at the hospital of another doctor. When called to ask why he was duplicating the X-rays and putting my father through another exhausting ordeal, the doctor said he wanted his own set of X-rays. This same doctor, by the way, refused to take calls from me, telling my father he preferred to deal directly with him.

Following up on the primary care doctor's orders, a hospice agency called to arrange an interview with my brother about my father's long-term care. But it was not the hospice agency the assisted living facility requested and which the doctor supposedly agreed to use.

Then there was the social worker who called from the Visiting Nurse Association (VNA) assigned to my dad, offering to help in any way she could. I called her back, leaving a message that the family was exhausted from running to all the doctors, and did she have any suggestion for transportation support. She never returned my call.

Six months into the constant grind of caring for two elderly and disabled parents, my brother summed it up best: The only efficient ones are the billing departments. They know exactly what's going on. They know exactly what to bill you for and when—sometimes twice.

It's time to put the care back into health, and forget the so-called "management."

Personal Responsibility

Self-responsibility is a principle of self-esteem. People who take respon-sibility for their personal growth experience higher self-esteem than those who do not.

—Adele Wilcox, *Self and Soul*

As my father's health began to decline, I helped out a great deal. I especially tried to be a sounding board for my brother who, because of his closer proximity to my parents, was carrying most of the burden.

"It all evens out," a friend told me once when I explained that I felt guilty. "You did a lot of the care-taking work when you were younger."

Still, my brother was the one who ran daily trips to nursing homes, hospitals, and the assisted-living facility. During a five-month period my parents were moved nine times between them. Each time, my brother—who has medical proxy for my father and legal guardianship for my mother—had to sign them into their new living situation. Once he even drove my mother to a psychiatric ward when he found her putting her feet in cereal bowls instead of shoes, and screaming "Liverpool, England!" for no apparent reason. When my father was taken to the hospital, my mother had forgotten to take her medicine and needed to be stabilized. Anyone else may have waited for an ambulance. My brother wanted to forego the unnecessary humiliation of a neighborhood nosey for news.

My brother also single-handedly cleaned out my parents' house and readied it for sale. I dealt with placing the advertisements, answering all the telephone inquiries, writing the brochure, showing the house to prospects and eventually securing a realtor.

Whenever my brother asked me to do something, like make a phone call or pick up a supply, I gladly assisted—grateful that he did so much.

My brother and I worked harder than anyone I know to secure a safe living situation for both our parents.

But there's one thing we could not do.

We couldn't make my father well, and we couldn't in the end give him the quality of life we both thought he more than earned.

My father rapidly became too ill to enjoy the many amenities of the luxury facility in which he lived.

The day I realized I couldn't "save" my father, even if I worked myself to the bone, I began to feel free. My father chose to wait until he was seventy-eight to retire. He chose to live at his home until his health failed. He chose to let my mother live an isolated life on the living room sofa.

We all have personal responsibility. I could only make my life choices, not his, not my husband's, not my friends', not even my children's. In the end, I chose to support my father by clarifying his health needs, sending him cards, calling him frequently, and visiting enough to see him—without devastating me or my own family.

I also chose to care for myself throughout his decline. I asked for help. I hired babysitters to relieve me of the dual demands of caretaking elderly parents and young children. I accepted my husband's offers to drive my father, who was too heavy for me to lift should he fall, to many of his doctor visits. I gave myself permission throughout the ordeal to be alone to cry, to vent my frustrations, and to nap when I felt exhausted. I tried to eat healthily to keep a stressful situation in check as much as possible.

Still, I had many moments of not holding it all together. My kids were yelled at more than they should have been, especially after I had spent four or five hours on the phone trying to verify medical information when all they wanted to do was play. Many nights when I tucked my daughter in I apologized, explaining it is difficult watching a parent get old and sick. The next day after such conversations, my daughter always seemed happier. She was grateful to hear the truth, especially hearing me own responsibility for my behavior.

Distance/Self-Preservation

True giving is an overflowing of your love. You don't feel that you are being depleted when you give in this way. In fact, you feel energized, because the love you give away returns to you through the gratitude of the people you have touched.

—Paul Ferrini, *Everyday Wisdom*

I used to think my husband was a bit cold-hearted when he didn't rush to his mother's side every time she was brought to the hospital or her doctor over the last four years of her life.

"It's self-preservation," my husband explained at the time. He had just begun a labor-intensive business, and we had two small and very dependent children to support. He was running on empty.

My husband once gave up his life to help his mother and his brother, who has Down's Syndrome. At twenty-eight, he gave himself permission to leave his mother's home and purchase his own home, which he said was the most liberating decision of his life.

The shoe was now on the other foot, and after experiencing great sadness each time I saw my father, I decided to put some distance between us. I called Dad and sent him cards. I just couldn't see him more than once every week or two. Some days it took me two and one half hours to get back home. I could have driven to another state in that time.

"Who says we have to be by someone's side when they are dying?" my friend Dijana asked me when I told her of my anger and guilt over my father's failing health. Earlier that year, when I knew he was dying even when the doctor's wouldn't confirm it, she encouraged me to be sure that I shared any unsaid thoughts with my

110

father. On numerous occasions I told him I loved him and thanked him for teaching me kindness.

Before I chose to give myself a break from the wrenching sight of his body rotting before my eyes, I was so stressed I wasn't there for anyone—not my husband, my children, my friends, or myself. Did my standing before him trying to appear brave help? His health certainly didn't improve because of it.

Is it the frequency of our visits or the quality of our relationship that matter the most in the end?

Secrets

Telling someone the truth alleviates the tension among the living as well as the dying.

—Martin Shepard, *Dying*

The anxiety returned, not in full force, but enough to have left me feeling off-center. Lying awake at night, agonizing over why I'd returned to the state of a frightened young child, I reprimanded myself for not functioning at a higher level. I was smart enough as a young child—top of my class—to accomplish anything. On this day I was afraid to go the grocery store. What happened to the strong, competent woman I know I am?

Instead, I wallowed again in the unbearable loneliness of growing up without the nurturance of a mother. Aching to feel safe, grounded, and supported, I cried hysterically. *Help me move beyond this paralysis of pain engulfing my every move,* I prayed.

Hours later the phone rang. As if she intuitively knew I hit rock bottom again, Dijana called me to say hi.

"I'm a mess," I muffled into the phone, embarrassed and relieved to have an objective sounding board. "All the anxiety is coming back and I don't understand why."

After explaining the care-taking issues of my dying father, she immediately pinpointed the source of my angst. No one, to the best of my knowledge, had told my father he would die soon. Carrying that secret—like the other more shameful ones about my father being an alcoholic and my mother being a schizophrenic, that I held in as a child—was making me feel crazy.

112

That the doctors—his primary care physician, his oncologist, and his gastroenterologist—continued to treat him as if he is going to be fine, when X-rays show that the cancer has spread to the lymph nodes seemed ludicrous.

"Maybe next year when I feel better I'll go with you to Nova Scotia," my father told me. I cringed, thinking to myself there would be no next year for him.

Did he not know or not want to face the truth, this man who had lived a life wrought with denial?

"I wish I could help you. I would, if I won the lottery," he told us on numerous occasions. My brother and I later found out that my father had an enormous savings account.

"This is just teenage conflict between a daughter and mother," he told me when I tried to explain my mother's irrational behavior. "Stop making up stories," he'd say when I'd tell him she was hiding behind the bushes watching me play tennis. Three months later my mother tried to kill herself.

Hiding truth hurts, as does someone's refusal to accept truth, and knowing the truth was not being spoken by those in authority to speak it seemed insane. Who is being protected by denial? No one I know in this situation.

My father was living in an assisted-living facility when he belonged in a hospital with round-the-clock care. Instead, my brother and I were called continuously with requests for diapers, prescriptions, and frequent rides to my father's doctor appointments, sometimes as often as twice a week. One day a nurse called simply to tell me that my mother had called 911 after my father fell off their sofa. Another time the resident manager took me aside to tell me about all the feces on the floor of my parents' apartment. My father couldn't make it to the bathroom in time anymore.

Yes, I was having difficulty coping with my father's imminent death because I was unable to provide the solace a dying person needs. I couldn't console a man who hadn't been given permission to grieve his own death.

"Forget the doctors," my friend advised. "The doctors' jobs are to keep people alive. You need to tell the hospice workers to give you some emotional support around this," she advised me.

Letting Go

For what I am suggesting threatens patriarchal society. Must not children honor their parents and care for them in old age? No, that was the very premise that made King Lear a tragedy ... The old are put on earth to nurture the young—not vice versa ... Of course, as we reach middle age we should help our parents help themselves. But we should help our parents out of gratitude and not at the cost of our own development. If we are to go down with the Titanic, let us give our places in the lifeboat to our children, not our parents.

—George Vaillant, *Aging Well*

Actively involved in the caretaking of my schizophrenic mother for more than thirty years, I finally reached a breaking point. My brother has handled all my mother's paperwork and basic shopping needs. I managed the calls from the assisted-living facility where she lived, and dealt with the doctors and care managers.

I received many calls with news like my mother was found wandering the halls harassing the night staff, or that my mother had spread feces all over her bathroom walls. Another time she allegedly shoved an aide who was trying to dress her.

My mother, on the other hand, would tell me that people were stealing her clothes or entering her room in the middle of the night.

One Thursday evening my mother's neuropsychologist called to tell me he would no longer work with my mother. He said he felt he had done all he could for her and that my mother now needed someone simply to take her out once in a while. "And your mother could benefit from a visit with you," he said. "Maybe you could take her out for scallops (her favorite meal) if not because you are her daugh-

114

ter, than for humanitarian reasons." I got defensive and began explaining all the times I did see her. When I hung up the phone, I was in a rage.

Who was this man, this doctor, to tell me to become more involved with my mother, a woman he barely knew? The rage broke me. I reached the point of no return when I recognized that I had suffered enough and could not for one second more continue living as "the good daughter."

Coached by a therapist, I resigned from all my care-taking duties. My counselor warned me, based on his experience from working several years on a psychiatric ward, that my mother could go either way: she could choose to kill herself, which was her responsibility, or she could rise to the occasion. I called together the team of six professionals involved in my mother's care and told them that I'd continue to be involved in the business decisions of my mother's care, but that physically and emotionally, I would no longer spend Saturday nights shopping for clothes my mother refused to wear or drive ninety minutes through Boston traffic to see a woman who refused to leave her ice cream at the dining room table to greet her daughter. I hired a private social worker to help with my mother's socialization by visiting her twice a month. I checked in on my mother by calling occasionally and visiting a couple times a year.

I explained that taking care of a mentally ill relative is different than supervising a physically ill parent. Others may view my mother as an elderly woman with a brain disease, but to me she has acted like a terrorist during many of my younger years, chasing me around the house with a vacuum cleaner, calling my teachers and harassing them, screaming at me for stepping on a nail by accident, stabbing my father in the back with a fork and throwing him down a flight of stairs, and standing up in a restaurant and singing "Happy birthday, you son of a bitch" to a woman in a nearby table whom she'd never met before. For these and many other reasons, I will never feel safe alone in a room with my mother. I will never know for sure if my mother will be stable or insane, if she took her medication or not, if she accepts me or rejects me. The torment of living with that fright is more exhausting than the demands of her physical needs.

Seven lives—those of my family and my brother's family— could no longer be sacrificed for one, I told the roomful of professionals. I owe it to my children to be there for them.

At the end of my speech, my mother's psychiatrist turned to the group and said, "Georgie [my mother] is not the only victim here. Gail is a victim, too. We need to help Gail heal now." I could have cried. Finally, someone heard me!

* * *

It's been eighteen months since I "let go" of my mother. I learned I cannot fix my mother, nor could I even console her. I had to make choices based on what I could give now. I will give my children a loving home. I will teach classes and counsel my clients one on one in moving beyond their pasts to create fulfilling lives. I will pray that my mother finds peace, but I can not give it to her. I did not cause her illness, and I have done more than enough to support her through her many crises, including hours of attending group therapy sessions with her as a teenager when I should have been out exploring the world. I would not sacrifice my family or myself any longer.

My mother is safe, which is a huge accomplishment for my brother and I, who worked nearly full-time for more than one year untangling red tape and court systems to give her a fine home. Others are not so fortunate. Schizophrenics reportedly comprise an estimated 30 percent of Boston's homeless community.

Giving up my mother's caretaking was a difficult choice. At first the freedom was terrifying. I felt guilt and shame about reclaiming my life as my own, not my mother's. I thought for sure my mother would die if I were not more vigilant about her care. The opposite has occurred. In freeing myself, I freed my mother. My mother now participates in activities she would not join before, such as riding the elder van to local shopping excursions and attending concerts at her assisted-living facility.

All the energy I focused on my mother's care is now redirected at my family and my career. I use my existence to express God's purpose for me, rather than use my mother as an excuse not to pursue my calling of helping adults in transition. It takes more courage to follow the latter path; it means I respond to the world as a competent woman, versus a frightened child trying to please Mommy.

And I want to teach other caregivers, women in particular, that sometimes they need to say "no" for their own sanity. Putting themselves and their children first is not selfish; it's self-preservation.

George Valliant explains the need for self-care more forcefully in his book, *Aging Well.* "I once made a study of men and women admitted to a medical/surgical hospital to understand the underlying psychological reasons why they come to the hospital *at this time.* No women were admitted to the hospital from the exhaustion of caring for multiple young children, but several women were admitted from the exhaustion of caring for ailing parents. Biology flows downhill."

PARENTS: EASE THE BURDEN

Do not leave loose ends.

- Organize all your paperwork and let your children know where to find important documents.

- Hire an estate planning lawyer and be sure to devise a will that you keep up to date to reflect any changes in your life.

- Know that your children are trying to help through a maze of confusion and uncertainty; be appreciative.

- Understand that as much as your children may love you, you cannot always be the center of their universe. Your children have many other professional and personal demands on their time.

IV. COPING WITH DEATH

This section is dedicated, for better AND worse, in loving memory of my dad, Waino J. Kauranen, who inadvertently gave me Sisu.

SISU

Sisu is much more than fortitude. It's an old characterization used by the Finnish people, maybe for the last ten thousand years.

Jean Sibelius once likened sisu to a metaphysical shot in the arm which makes a man (or woman) do the impossible ... the mystifying four letters ... as something that surpasses fearlessness ... an extraordinary endurance, a kind of inner fire or superhuman nerve force which includes courage, tenacity, stubborn determination, energy, and a will (and ability) to get things done.

Introduction

The death of a loved one is, for most of us, the most profound emotional experience we will ever have to endure. Dealing with the deep and prolonged grief that follows such a loss may well be the most painful and disturbing challenge of our lives.

—Carol Staudacher, *A Time to Grieve: Meditations for Healing After the Death of a Loved One*

There is one birth every eight seconds and one death every thirteen seconds, according to the U.S. Census Bureau's statistics as of November 26, 2001.

Despite its inevitability, death catches most of us off-guard. We are not taught that moving through grief is a life-transforming process, not the three-day bereavement period companies often grant employees.

A typical grieving period can last one to two years for a "normal death," in which there were no unusual circumstances such as murder or suicide, according to Dr. Vamik D. Volkan, author of *Life After Loss: The Lessons of Grief.*

To complicate matters, we all grieve differently, depending upon our personality, our sex, and our relationship with the loved one. My husband and my brother ran around like maniacs "getting things done" after losing a parent, which to me resembled some typical male "problem-solving" behavior. Yet grief cannot be solved—it must be felt. A spiritual friend of mine advised that these men were indeed probably hurting. "An animal in pain runs," she said. Another therapist friend wisely told me, "Let them do whatever they have to do to get through the process."

120

At first I was numb and withdrawn after losing my father—not exactly a productive step forward either. In fact, the work of grief often means taking a major step inward and letting go of any major external efforts for a long time.

Another friend said she was so upset about losing her mother that she felt as if she were experiencing post-traumatic stress syndrome. It takes time to absorb the initial shock before embracing the subsequent healing, which is probably why grief experts recommend that those who have lost a loved one make no major changes in their life for at least one year.

Feeling our way through grief sometimes occurs much later when we are not so busy trying to settle an estate, console other relatives, and catch up on all the work we missed when caring for the dying person.

A cousin of mine said she was strong at her mother's funeral. She even orchestrated a sit-down meal for all those who came to comfort her. Six months later, at a neighbor's wake, she cried uncontrollably and left embarrassed. "I realized I was so busy with school and organizing my mother's funeral that I had not yet grieved her death. At my neighbor's wake I was finally able to feel the loss of my own mother," she said.

Even when we come to accept the sadness of a death, many of us are not ready for the other feelings—like anger—that come forth. As William Bridges so eloquently explains in his book, *The Way of Transition*, "The old resentments and hurts make mourning the person doubly hard."

In the following section I lead you, the reader, through the grief and mourning of my father, who raised me by himself through much of my life. When he died I felt like I lost both a mother and a father on the same day and any sense of roots. I felt orphaned.

According to Clea Simon, author of *Fatherless Women*, nearly half of women before the age of fifty will lose their fathers.

The work of moving forward and healing is two-fold. As Bridges clarifies: "'Grieving' comes from an ancient root-word meaning 'heavy' and refers to the feeling that accompanies a loss. 'Mourning,' on the other hand, comes from a root-word referring to 'remembering.' The latter therefore deals more with the way that the mind works on the broken connection, while the former deals more with the sadness and depression that is the result of the break."

The death of a loved one is an initiation for the mourner into another way of being. For those of us who have lost a parent it may mean that we finally have to grow up and find the wholeness within what we had sought from the deceased.

Grief

Death is still a fearful, frightening happening, and the fear of death is a universal fear, even if we think we have mastered it on many levels.

—Elisabeth Kubler-Ross, *On Death and Dying*

I couldn't imagine that the day my father died would be more painful than the last six months I had watched his body deteriorate and his mind slip into states of confusion.

With the terminally ill person you really lose them long before he or she dies. When I went into my backyard, I knew that my father would never again be sitting by the pool watching his grandchildren swim. I cried.

When I thought of our vacation in Cape Cod and I remembered the times my father sat with us there, I cried.

When I talked to him on the phone—usually by shouting, because he couldn't hear me too well—I wondered if it would be our last conversation. I always told him I loved him before hanging up.

When I saw him struggle to stand or walk, I stiffened to remind myself to be strong in his presence. I also tightened up in front of my children, postponing my tears until I was alone in bed.

"There comes a point when you pray that every breath is his last," a neighbor told me about watching her father die after a long illness. I understood. The frail man who slept all day or became easily angered when awake was not the person I remembered my father to be. I wanted to connect to his spirit, his smile, his laughter, and his silliness. I wanted my memories to be of his love and kindness, not of his frail body. I needed to forgive all my father's shortcomings and send him love, to ask no more of him, and to let him rest and be comforted.

Every time the phone rang, I thought it's "the call" telling me my father had passed away. It was hard to make any plans, at least not any too far from home. I didn't feel too much like socializing, yet I couldn't postpone my own family's lives. My children wanted play dates, food on the table, and hugs and kisses too. My husband had a business to run, even though he'd graciously made himself available to help take my father to his many appointments.

The stress of being torn in so many directions was sometimes hard to handle. Little tasks, like returning a library book, seemed monumental. I wanted to retreat and be grounded in my home. I needed to regroup from caring so much for so many and connect with my soul for a few minutes.

My soul wanted to learn to accept death as another chapter. I needed to know I would always be connected to my father through memories—the whale watch one summer, dining by the docks at Marina Bay, and seeing my kids riding their bikes on the driveway my father had paved for us.

Death is like birth, full of innocence. When my mother-in-law passed away, I could remember only the good in her. Her flaws disappeared. With my father approaching death, I saw only a man who cared for his wife and worked all his life. His lapses into irresponsibility seemed minor. His difficult life seemed huge and sad.

I honored him in my own life by expressing the kindness he taught me. His illnesses taught both my brother and I to live healthy and in the present.

Retirement doesn't give us freedom. We choose freedom by accepting only those responsibilities that are ours.

My dad chose to protect my mother all his life. I honored him for attempting to manage such an impossible and an arduous task. I pitied him for not seeking help along the way.

Enough

Most people are nicer to total strangers than they are to their loved ones and to themselves.

—Wayne W. Dyer, *Pulling Your Own Strings*

The times when I don't operate at 100 percent efficiency are the most difficult for me. I remember as a young girl when I was frustrated about not being able to do a task my mother would say, "Never say you can't." And for many years, through super achievement and super responsibility, I didn't. I excelled in perfect attendance, high honor grades, staying quiet, and never asking for help.

Vulnerability was not tolerated in my mother's presence; she couldn't handle it. As a result, I learned two false beliefs that continued to crop up during every crisis of my life. One, I am a burden if I have a need. Two, I am not enough if I'm not always putting my best self forward.

As a young adult I felt I was not enough because I couldn't cure my mother's schizophrenia. I couldn't even tolerate her.

Later, no one else in my life was enough either—not my husband, my friends, or any of my ex-boyfriends, because none could take away my pain of losing a mother to a devastating and shameful mental illness. Only I could release the pain by feeling it.

Watching my father die, I didn't want to cook, shop, or entertain friends. I couldn't be "on." I was sad. I needed private space to grieve.

At the time I was not the best spouse, mother, friend, daughter, or sister. I felt human, and I was hurting. I also felt like that was OK.

125

I permitted myself to be less giving to others now so I could recharge my own stretched resources.

"This is just a phase," my friend Bess reminded me. "A year from now you'll feel differently and you'll look back and won't even remember being so vulnerable."

Enough is a harsh judgment and I've been the toughest critic of all.

DOs AND DON'Ts OF DYING

Tell the truth, no matter what.

• Doctors never told my father he was dying, even though it was evident to all those who loved him. Pretending all was OK when it clearly was not was a tough game for all of us to play, and in the end, it served no one. The inevitable happened. Looking back, I would have comforted my father in other ways had we freely been able to discuss his impending death. I surely would have held his hand more, stroked his head, encouraged him to rest, and told him he put up a great fight. And I would have kept asking for him to pass on more of his many gems of wisdom. I'd also want to know more about his life, particularly his Finnish roots, his World War II experience, his youth, and his marriage to my mother. Instead of being by his side, I spent hours outside in doctors' waiting rooms and on the phone verifying appointments which served little purpose other than give false hope to a dying patient.

• Tell the grandchildren, no matter what their age, the truth about their ill loved one. Children sense when someone is not himself or herself; validate their knowing. It was my daughter, eight years old at the time, who said to me one day after we brought my father on our annual whale watching trip. "Mom, I don't think Papa will be going on that trip with us next year." I told her I thought she may be right. Her Papa is very ill and he may die soon. He did not survive until the next trip.

• Show your authentic emotions. Teach children that it is OK—in fact, quite normal—to cry when you are losing someone you love. I remember reading in a book about preparing children for grief to tell them you are emptying your bucket of tears. To this day, my daughter will say, "Mom, are you finished emptying your bucket of tears?" At first I'd tell her it was half empty. Then, on certain occasions like my father's birthday, I'd tell her there were a few tears left. It was comforting for her to see me progress through grief.

• Acknowledge that children experience loss, even if they cannot express it. Let children, if they choose to, participate in the funeral proceedings so they, too, can begin to put closure on the loss of a loved one.

• Read *Talking with Children About Loss* by Maria Trozzi.

Endings

I have often thought the term "normal grief" was a contradiction in terms; there is little normal about grief. To lose a compelling person in our lives is agonizing. Our reactions, dreams, or daydreams, laced with anger, denial and splitting, may seem downright weird. Such responses in the first weeks or months after death or loss are typical symptoms of grief, as hallucinations accompanying a high fever are common. Difficult to endure, to be sure, but not in themselves a sign of madness.

—Vamik D. Volkan and Elizabeth Zintl, *Life After Loss*

My father died August 2, 2000, with my brother, my husband, and myself by his side.

First, the nurse from his assisted-living facility called early in the morning to tell me my father was taken by ambulance to a near-by hospital. He'd been taken numerous times over the past several weeks, so it wasn't an unusual event. It took half a day to figure out which hospital he was sent to. Then the call came early in the after-noon, warning me that the day would probably be my father's last.

"Gail, I don't how to prepare you for this, so I'm just going to say it," my brother calmly spoke into the phone after meeting with two of my father's doctors at the hospital. "Dad's on his way out. There's nothing you or I can do. He probably won't make it through the night."

I cried, understanding fully that the day I'd been dreading my entire life had arrived. Nothing happened the way I expected it to after that. Rushing to my dad's bedside, I watched my father strug-gle, eyes closed, through his last breaths of life. My brother held his hand, told him he loved him, and stroked his hair. I was so touched by my brother's gentleness, this sibling of mine, 6' 5", caring for his father as tenderly as one would a newborn baby. Then my brother asked me if I wanted to hold my father's hand. I did. I told my father that I was there. No response, but I knew he knew. Then I asked my husband if he, too, wanted to share in our handholding ritual. He did. We all watched as my dad tossed and turned, mumbling, "I'm tired. It's the ninth inning." I remember thinking to myself, *Dad you should be tired. You put up such a good fight, demanding to the end to live, despite your inability to walk, hear well, stand, or even eat. You tried, against the odds of cancer, diabetes, asbestosis, blocked arteries, cirrhosis of the liver, to live. You tried to protect Mom and Wayne and me from your death, never fully admitting you were dying. It's OK to move on now. It's selfish of me to ask you to hang on one more minute so I can hear your kind voice once more tell me you love me and my family. I've got to let you go.*

About a half hour later, after watching my father thrash about in his hospital gown, my husband and I left for dinner. My brother went for a ride. We all needed a break from this wrenching scene, which could continue on throughout the night. When we returned, the nurse asked us to wait outside my father's room for a while. Then a male nurse came out and told us my father had passed. We reentered his room. My brother, my husband, and I embraced one another and stood by my dad. I kissed him goodbye. It was peaceful. Death was not the scary demon I thought it to be. I felt enormous gratitude that I was loved by such a dear man. It was that love that let me send him on his way, to be comforted and embraced. Then, I felt a huge sense of relief; the suffering was over.

Grief was another story. Private, exhausting, quiet, painful, and pure, grief is sneaky, choosing to appear at the most unexpected moments. Funeral tears are so much more formal than the primal ones that come gushing forth in the middle of the night or at the memory of a word he spoke, a gesture he did, a presence he had.

The three days of bereavement time off corporations give employees covers the period of playing hostess to friends and family through death itself, not the healing process.

A month later, the finality of my father's death hit me.

At first, surrounded by children still home for summer vacation and the needs of my newly widowed mother, I would cry only sporadically. I had days of feeling numb and detached, moments of a panicky off-centeredness, followed by a flood of raw tears ripping out from the center of my chest as if my heart were literally breaking apart.

I was irritable at the hectic pace of life and the people who needed me. I wanted to be alone. Yet it was those people who needed me that made sense of my life without my dad.

I was angry that the world wouldn't stop when I hurt. I was angry that no one could heal my new pain, the deep sense of loss.

I also had moments of real joy, relieved that my father had smiled so much. It reminded me now to find happiness within, to be grateful that my best friend was by my side, to be happy that I reconnected with my brother and my father's family.

Other times the vulnerability of loss would set in. I'd be walking along and need to hold onto something or someone for fear I'd fall. I was scared to be left alone. A couple of times I would reach for my husband's hand. Twice, feeling shaky and light-headed, I called upon grace to get me through the moment and help me safely home.

Perhaps nature deals us grief in spurts so we can continue to function while we absorb the enormity of a loss. Reorganizing life without the physical presence of a loved one takes time.

Courage

Consistently choosing safety over adventure, brakes over accelerator, no over yes, and consistently preferring to be a passive observer rather than an active participant in our own lives can readily bring anger and remorse, sorrow and frustration ... Not honoring ourselves is fatefully tied up with not honoring others: our children and partners, our communities, the natural world. All of them suffer from our passivity and judgment.

—Greg Levoy, *Callings*

"I don't believe in God," my mother told me the morning my brother and I stopped by to tell her my father had died. I didn't blame her. My mother prayed most of her life that God take her before my dad. She became so dependent upon my father that she could not imagine managing without him. God didn't answer her prayer in the way she wanted.

In my late teens, I also prayed frantically that God would help me. Not take me, but take me from my frightening mother to a safe place. When I wasn't removed from my home to some loving and compassionate arms, it was hard for me, too, to believe that God existed.

I have since learned that we don't find God by relying on others. We find God when we take all of those courageous steps of relying on ourselves.

By circumstances of being widowed, my mother began taking giant strides every day. Her progress was miraculous. She bathed, dressed, answered the phone, dined alone, and even lightly cleaned her studio apartment. She did none of these actions when my father was alive.

"How do you account for your mother's miraculous break-throughs towards self-sufficiency and peace of mind?" numerous people asked me, as my brother and I watched in awe at my mother's leaps forward.

The standard response from many close to the situation has been that my father protected my mother too much, that the doctor overmedicated her for years, that she now feels safe in an assisted-living facility as opposed to alone in a big house for many solitary hours. All those answers have some truth to them.

But they didn't account for one major event: my mother choosing personal responsibility by changing her thought process, the private decision she made at some point to go forward. After she blew out her birthday candles in celebration of her seventy-second year, I asked what she wished for. "A happy rest of my life," she responded, smiling. The smile alone was incredulous.

No one had changed her medicine. She still rightfully grieved the death of my father. And she is living alone for the first time in forty-seven years. That she spoke her hope aloud is truly remarkable.

When we replace false beliefs of inadequacy with healthier thoughts of love and strength, not only does our world change, but the life around all those we care about improves, too. It's what healing does. When one person heals, everyone around them has the chance to heal.

For those of us who have lived much of life in pain, it takes courage to be happy. But if my mother—a grieving widow who endured shock treatments, psychiatric wards, disconnection from family and friends, and years lost to apathy and overmedication—can rise to the occasion, we all have the capability. Be brave.

EULOGY:
My Dad ... Farewell to a Humble Man

What comforts all of us in our loss is what I call the blessing of remembrance. After grief comes solace, the solace of remembering all that we enjoyed about our loved one.

—Ted Menton, *After Goodbye*

We don't hear too much about humility in this day of bigger, better, and more. Twenty-eight-year-old "dot-com" millionaires, a construction boom creating monstrous 6,000-square-foot homes with rooms nobody has any time to use, and a near 50 percent divorce rate make headlines instead. Ironically, we call these "prosperous times."

Here's a story about my father, a man who lived with less. He retired at seventy-eight, when his weary legs could no longer help him supervise the many construction sites for which he was responsible.

He was a gentle man, who for forty-seven years took care of his wife through the most tragic of mental illnesses: schizophrenia. He did not even tell his own doctors of the burdens he bore. Until the day he died, he insisted on being with my mother, demanding that a hospital or nursing home release him as soon as possible so he could be by his wife's side. In fact, the grief for most of us who knew my dad was this: he lost his life to my mother long before he died. He chose her over himself or anyone else.

"Everyone has a cross to bear," he would tell me, explaining you have to have faith. He carried his cross with a quiet dignity, finding joy in the simplest things. A perfect day for my dad was sitting by our kitchen table watching the birds eat from a feeder or teaching his grandson Steven how to use a new tool.

Looking at all the pictures of my dad, my brother commented, "There's not one picture where Dad isn't smiling or holding a baby on his lap."

When I was little and I looked into my dad's aqua blue eyes, I used to think I saw God, his kindness seemed so pure.

My dad used to take the neighborhood kids, my brother, and me out for huge ice cream sundaes. In later years, he took my mom. Sometimes he led a tribe of us on hikes through the Blue Hills Reservation. He was often silly, playing imaginary games with us. He'd tell my childhood friend, Paula, and me that his car could fly over telephone wires. The stone building by the Braintree Reservoir was Porky Pig's house, according to him.

Patient to a fault, he once waited at Logan Airport—without checking with the airlines first about delays—eight hours to pick up my friend Bess and me on a return trip from Cancun, Mexico. He also drove my high school sweetheart to college in Washington, D.C., plowing his way slowly through a major snowstorm down the Eastern seacoast. He spent endless hours on the phone listening to my brother or me sort through a problem. He loved our spouses as if they were his own children.

The encouraging gems of wisdom he offered at the most spontaneous moments often showed me he understood where I was in my life, sometimes better than I. The day I arrived at my first job out of college as a cub reporter, the city editor handed me a letter. "The Gazette is lucky to have you," my dad wrote, signing it from "the beach ball with legs," a name my mom used to tease him with as he grew to be 250 pounds.

Another time, sad that I wasn't married in my twenties, he said to me, "Good waiters get good tips."

Later, when I was unsure about who I was dating, he'd say, "Marry a happy man."

I did, and a few years later when I became a mother, he said to me, "You know how much you love your daughter Catie? That's how much I love you."

His greatest love, though, was his wife, Georgie. "We used to have so much fun. She was a wonderful girl," he told my husband recently en route to a doctor's appointment. Despite his frail health, he refused to die until my mother was comfortably settled into her new and safe home, a beautiful assisted-living facility where my mother was treated with respect and given lots of support.

My father was a good person who helped many in his lifetime. He loved children and decent people, and always rooted for the underdog. A great man passed on, but his lessons continue: love, kindness, and family first.

MANAGING GRIEF

Don't be a martyr. Take care of yourself.

• Nature heals. Spend as much time as you can in calm, soothing surroundings. Avoid loud, chaotic places like shopping malls that can add to the stress you may be feeling.

• Give yourself private time every day to sit quietly. Honor whatever emotions appear. Know that anxious feelings are common in grief; don't unnecessarily meditate or drink them away. You need to feel them to release the emotions, as painful as they can be.

• Share your feelings with a trusted friend. A spouse who has not yet lost a loved one may not be able to give you the same level of comfort and reassurance as an acquaintance who has experienced grief.

• Know that even if family and friends surround you, you can feel lonely. Grief is an individual journey.

• Lean on others. Delegate responsibilities like grocery shopping and childcare for a while to give yourself time to regroup.

• Understand that grief may happen in spurts. One day you may feel like you're over the death, and the next you may not even want to get out of bed. On a particularly tough day of feeling sad or lonely, pull out all the cards you received after your loved one died and reread them for support.

• Read *A Time to Grieve* by Carol Staudacher, *Life After Loss* by Dr. Vamik D. Volkan, *The Way of Transition* by William Bridges, *After Good-Bye* by Ted Menton, or *Losing a Parent* by Alexandra Kennedy.

Private Hell

Despair is a time of waiting, of paralysis, of non-time ... Despair is the experience among others that is incomplete, something that has not yet become itself, a creature not yet formed out of the murk and waters.

—John Tarrant, *The Light Inside the Dark*

"It took a year to start feeling normal again after the death of my dad," a friend who lost her father several years ago told me.

I asked her, "Did you feel numb and off center a lot?"

"Oh, yes. It was the hardest year of my life," she told me.

I responded, "It's hell. A private hell."

"You're right. No one can go through this for you. You have to deal with the pain by yourself. The world all around continues on like nothing happened, but you're in pain," she explained.

I concurred, telling her it was hard for me to watch my husband return from work smiling when I was hurting so deeply inside. My father was dead and buried, and I'd grieved a month, so I was supposed to move forward and act like nothing happened? I moved, all right, trembling inside, determined to get beyond the anguish of grief. I walked, talked, yelled, and screamed through it, too. It hurt.

I was irritable. I wanted to yell, "I lost a father, a best friend. Be gentle with me."

What I really needed was to be gentle with myself.

It hurt that he was gone. It hurt to reevaluate my relationship with him and unravel the unhealthy parts so I could find some healing in his death. Old wounds I thought I'd buried with my dad resurfaced.

Death is but another transition, another chance at transformation. All sorts of conflicting emotions emerged. I missed him, yet I leaned on him too much. He leaned on me too much. Neither of us learned to cope alone. I found safety in caring for him instead of venturing forth myself. He used me to be the forerunner in many crisis situations, knowing I'd take care of things he wouldn't. Later, he used my brother to do the same.

He modeled dependency. Even as I embraced self-sufficiency, death brought me back into the well, that dark place from which we have to climb out of if we want to celebrate our wholeness. Revisiting those murky waters after experiencing the freedom of living with joy was tough.

I understood why sometimes people who lose a loved one remarry quickly. Many avoid feeling the pain and discomfort of the unknown and choose not to learn how to take care of themselves. They grab external security when internal peace seems unattainable.

I wanted my husband to take away all hurt, to make up for a childhood of inconsistent and unhealthy love. I withdrew when he ignored a request of mine, like my needs didn't matter. I screamed any time he did anything that made me feel unsafe, like drive too fast or yell too loud. I vented when he didn't listen to my point of view, when he insisted his perspective was accurate.

Healthy interdependence was what I needed. How did I create something I never saw modeled? When was it OK to ask for help and encouragement? When was it OK to receive support?

A Reality Check

But part of what makes mourning such hard work is that the ties you had with the lost one are woven of dark strands, as well as light ones.

—William Bridges, *The Way of Transition*

In life, my father was a saint to me. He could do no wrong. After all, he stayed with my mother—a despondent, hysterical, and frightening woman—and he stayed with my brother and me. I owed him "big time" for not abandoning us, I thought. I paid him back by parenting him in the way I really needed to be parented, forfeiting my childhood in the process. During times of my mother's many psychotic breakdowns when she was committed to yet another psychiatric ward and gone for weeks, I became a surrogate spouse to my father, listening and comforting him through the turmoil.

In grieving his death, I came to see another side of my dad, which was too scary to absorb as a young child, for if I saw the truth I would realize how alone I truly was in a house with two incompetent parents. Instead, I chose to make him "the good guy" who would save me from my crazy mother. I held him on a pedestal, cherishing every silly word he uttered.

Now I have found the courage to look at my father's darkness and its impact on me.

My father's drinking humiliated me. Two particularly painful incidents come to mind. The first was my freshman year at a small women's college in Washington, D.C., where I was one of the few students on financial aid. Susan Ford (along with all her security guards) was in my freshman class; at the time, her father was president of the United States. I chose the college to be close to my high

138

school sweetheart, who was attending a nearby university, and to get as far away from home as I could. Having come from a blue-collar background, I never quite fit in with my elite group of classmates, many of whom had been debutantes. I didn't even know what a debutante was until I went to college.

Anyway, my father came to visit me after spending an evening drinking with my boyfriend. I mistakenly told him that my room-mate was being evicted because she was found to be a kleptomaniac. Drunk, my father started saying things to her, and he got so out of hand that he had to be removed from my dormitory by the college guards. The next day I was called into the dean of students' office to discuss my father's behavior. I will remember that day as one of the most embarrassing of my life. At the end of the year, when I was presented my financial aid package, I did not receive enough assistance to return to the college the next year, even though I was an excellent student. I will never know if the incident with my father tainted the decision.

The second embarrassing moment was when my father totaled his car and was arrested for drunk driving. His name was broadcast on the local radio station. My father joked about the incident, laughing about the night he spent in jail. Whenever we drove past the police station he would say, "I spent a night there." Oddly, his laughter made me think his behavior was acceptable.

"We all have a dark side and a light side," a friend shared with me as I wrestled with my father's alcoholism. "He's neither all one way or the other." Removing my father from the pedestal of sainthood meant I had to save myself. We all need to. There's no outside source that lifts us from personal responsibility. It's a solo journey.

These more blatant examples of my father's dysfunction only hint at the pain he caused me. The worst of his sins—for which I have paid dearly by living years of my adult life in a constant state of anxiety—was leaving me alone in a house with an unsafe mother and expecting me to watch over her as she expressed suicidal tendencies. No fifteen-year-old child should be ever given that responsibility.

As I moved further along with accepting my father's death, I've had to embrace my own anger with my father for not protecting me—anger that was justified, anger that was real, anger that hurt.

In my younger adulthood, that anger fueled me forward, enabling me to take on great challenges. Now I'm feeling the pain, releasing the anger, and embracing the lessons I've learned:

•I no longer accept responsibilities that are not mine. It was my father's duty to watch my mother or see that she was properly supervised, not mine.

•I choose ways to honor and protect myself. Others may have abandoned me in the past, but I have the power now never again to abandon myself.

Easter Sunday, April 15, 2001
A Letter to Dad

It takes courage—this is often called the path of the Spiritual Warrior—to endure sharp pains of self-discovery rather than choose to take the dull pain of unconsciousness that would last the rest of our lives.

—Marianne Williamson, *A Return to Love*

Dear Dad,

It's Easter Sunday, my third holiday without you. Thanksgiving was the worst—your death was so new to me. Mom and I sobbed our way through the meal, hugging each other as we reminisced about you. It was one of my most special times with Mom, a bonding moment I would not think possible before your death. God's grace touched me that day, I know, because schizophrenics don't typically show emotion. Mom didn't even cry at her own parents' funerals. That brief connection gave me a false hope of a recovery for Mom. One week later, on what would have been your eightieth birthday, she descended to the hell of illusions again, and Wayne and I had to commit her to a psych ward. Still, for one of the most grief-stricken moments of my life, Mom was actually there and it was your death that brought us together.

You would be proud of Wayne and me, too, Dad. We're taking good care of Mom as her co-guardians, and we have become closer, like you always hoped we would. Mom is now living back at her own assisted-living apartment after a six-week stay at the psych unit. She's spending today with Wayne.

Your death has taught me much, Dad. For one, I know now that you were much wiser than I understood you to be when you were living. That you could smile, be patient, have faith, and live without complaint when all around you was falling apart seems incredulous.

The calm and gentleness I so admired in you are qualities I am trying to build into my life now. Your death made it mandatory that I look within for these traits instead of to you.

I've also had to grow up a lot, Dad. Until you passed from Earth, I thought you'd be there for me if I truly needed anything. Now I'm learning for the first time to trust myself. The safety net is gone. It's been such a scary time living in this world without the illusion of you as a crutch. I had many, many days when I was anxious and insecure. Yet, that needy part of me needed to die, too, Dad.

You helped give me a life. Now, I have to claim it as my own. That's an awesome responsibility. The loss of you forced me to live from my life purpose, as scared as I was to move forward and claim my identity. When I finally reached the depths in mourning six months after your death, I made a decision to pull myself up. We all have the choice of whether to live in love or fear. You chose love; Mom chose fear. I agonized at the crossroads for what seemed like an eternity before choosing to follow your footsteps, Dad. That choice to follow love returned me, at a much deeper and compassionate level, to my life's work of helping those in transition connect with themselves and one another. I am passionate about my work; it connects me to my soul and to God.

Two weeks before you died when I was talking about our upcoming vacation to the beach house you told me, "Go in the sand and play with the kids." I am forever conscious now of making sure I find time to be fully present to Catie and Brendan.

I've also had time to think about your flaws, because mourning doesn't just bring up the saint-like qualities. Your drinking and your laziness left me with lots of responsibilities that should have been yours. As much as I wept for the loss of you, I've raged at the many times you abandoned me. Healing those feelings of abandonment is an ongoing task for me, one of my greatest personal challenges. There are still days since you died when I enter a grocery store, mall, or any large, crowded place that I feel like a hysterical three-year-old child lost in an aisle without a parent to be found anywhere.

Yet when I look at your flaws, I see my own, too. I waited angrily for much of my adult life for you to make it all up to me. That anger kept me separate from you and others. I wanted love and acceptance, while privately shouting "Hands off! No one's ever going to hurt me that way again." It's time to heal that wound, too, allowing others to touch both my tender and strong parts. Most have only seen the tough exterior.

Dad, it's Easter, a time of rebirth. So, out with the old and in with the new. No more looking at each of our inadequacies. Instead, I want to experience the simplicities you understood so well and the silliness and laughter that were such a huge part of you.

* * *

Gary Zukav, author of *The Seat of the Soul*, says upon death the obit should read, "To be continued." I think in life we need to honor new scripts, too.

Nine-Month Progress

So perhaps the only choice we have is to choose what to do with our dead: To die when they die. To live crippled. Or to forge, out of pain and memory, new adaptations. Through mourning we acknowledge that pain, feel that pain, live past it.

—Judith Viorst, *Necessary Losses*

I'm not sure if it's a coincidence that like the length of pregnancy, it took me nine months to re-center myself after my father's death. I know for sure that a new me evolved through the grief.

In the beginning stages of letting go of my dad's physical presence in my life, I was so numb from stress I couldn't feel my legs. "I think I have multiple sclerosis," I would tell my husband. Yes, grief can be that debilitating, especially if you feel it and don't medicate it. Slowly, I began walking alone and prayed every step that I wouldn't fall with no one nearby to rescue me. My deepest abandonment wounds came forth, challenging every solo task.

The only place I felt safe to be alone was at home. I became a recluse at first. Slowly, I took short jaunts—to the library, to the post office. A one-mile loop felt safe, then two. One day I had to visit my parents' lawyer and drive through Boston alone. I cried through my fear the night before, feeling like a fragile five-year old instead of the adult woman I was. I have since learned from reading books on grief that these frightening feelings are not unusual. Some people stop driving forever after the death of the loved one. It's not the driving they fear; but rather the knowledge that they, too, could die. I was determined to move forward, despite these concerns for my own safety.

144

Some days I was able to handle long trips—other days I was not. Grief is not a smooth ride, but it is rather like a roller coaster. Still, I feel grounded in this new adult woman I've become.

The little girl who once suppressed her feelings through over-work and achievement is the adult woman who consciously chooses to set aside time each day to cry or be still. This week I had two bliss-ful moments of feeling grace, that peaceful inner feeling of floating.

Creating also helps me move forward. I hit despair this past winter when we committed my mother to a psych ward, only four months after my father had died. That second loss, seeing my moth-er plunge to lows I hadn't witnessed since I was fifteen years old, sank me into a depression that frightened me. When my husband and brother said as gently as they could, "You don't want to do to your children what your mother did to you, do you?" I knew I had to take action. I created a hugely successful workshop called Beyond Motherhood. By focusing on my higher purpose, the stressors in my life were lessened.

The place in my heart that felt ripped apart and lonely is start-ing to mend. I want to give again.

Grief is so stressful. One of my friends told me last September that she was feeling more self-confident than she had in years. In my mind I thought, "I am so shaky, I will never feel confident again."

While I'm starting to feel centered again, nothing is the same. I feel older, uglier, and lonelier. I'm worn out. Grief is exhausting. I've carried the heaviness of it in my slumped shoulders.

I am a different person than I was last year. I have a new calm, hard-earned from sleepless nights, feeling and releasing chronic anxiety into pillows soaked with tears and talking about how much I miss my dad. I am grateful for any act of kindness shown to me, more alert to simple pleasures, and appreciative of anything that feels solid and secure after enduring the feeling of having the ground beneath my feet blown away. I am less tolerant of superficial values and more conscious of my own mortality.

I've had a few laughs and lots of joyful cuddle times with my children. Hurting moments have become healing ones. We all plant-ed flowers at my dad's grave. Sobbing, I felt his presence for the first time since he passed on. He was happy and smiling, glad his grand-children were there. Rituals, like visiting his grave, have become important to us.

One evening over dinner my son said, "Papa must be very hungry down there. All he has to eat is dirt and rocks." The innocence of children brings me back to the present. My dad wanted me to be a good mother, not a grieving daughter. Moving on and cherishing life are what I will want for my children, too, when I die.

Letting go of grief doesn't mean I don't honor and love my dad; it just means I also need to honor my family and myself.

Dad, peace to us all. I love you.

An Inward Year

Fill your life with people you trust and who are capable of enacting relationships based on giving and receiving. Pick a work place with like-minded others and link up with folks of similar values.

—Gail McMeekin, *The Power of Positive Choices*

I have deemed the year following my father's death "an inward year," a time for re-centering and recharging. A further cleansing of my past took place and a deeper connection to myself and God occurred.

I did most of my healing in isolation, not by choice, but because that is the nature of my work as a writer and personal and business coach. Looking back, I wish I had a job to go to on a daily basis for some structure and a sense of community. I was reminded of my early days as a new mother when the isolation was also painful and uncomfortable.

Two people helped me through my grief without even knowing it: my personal trainer and my physical therapist. I decided to use some money from my inheritance to hire a personal trainer, not just to get in shape, but to have some place to release my anxiety from grief. Meeting weekly with Lisa at her home, even on days I didn't want to get out of bed, helped me move forward. I had a safe place to go that was just for me. Self-care is crucial to mending any broken heart.

The other person who provided stability was my physical therapist, Paul. Six months after my father died, I woke up one morning with a painful left shoulder and the inability to lift my arm. Visits to my general practitioner confirmed I had a "frozen shoulder"—an

ADVICE ON HEALING THE HURT

Connect to the loved one who passed away.

• Visit the gravesite or some other memorial you have established.

• Write letters to the deceased periodically. Tell him or her about your life now, ask questions about issues you are unsure of, and forgive both yourself and the deceased for misunderstandings or imperfections if you are ready.

• Instill within yourself the qualities you admired in the loved one who died.

• Find ways the loss has transformed your life for the better. Have you become stronger, more independent, more spiritual, more loving, or more accepting? Did you question the meaning of your life or the quality of your relationships since your loved one passed away? What will you teach your children about death? What would the loved one that died want you to teach your children about death?

odd ailment that typically affects women in their forties and fifties. At first I resented going for my twice-weekly visits to physical therapy as prescribed. I didn't want to take the time. Yet those visits also gave a structure to my life during a very shaky year.

I learned from both Lisa and Paul, two very positive people, to accept nurturance. I was so grateful to be able to receive, after a frantic year of giving every ounce of myself to caretaking elderly parents.

These professional connections led me to continue finding ways of building a sense of community for myself so I would no longer need to focus on my lack of extended family. I started a book group with a friend of mine, joined a mom-to-mom group at a local church, and wrote to other writers via e-mail.

While we need to go inward sometimes to grow, it's not safe to stay in isolation too long.

Freedom

But in retrospect, I see the loss of my father as a crucial factor in my growth, in my ability to finally walk away from childish ways that no longer served me or my family ... That for many of us, somehow, the loss of our fathers triggered changes and brought about a time of growth that helped us realize fullness in our lives.

—Clea Simon, *Fatherless Women*

"You never completely get over it," my uncle told me a few months after my father died, when I was frustrated at myself for still wallowing in grief. At the time, I remember mornings standing in the backyard waiting for our new puppy to relieve himself. I'd look at the tall trees surrounding our house and think to myself, *Dad, I don't feel like I'll ever stand tall again. I feel like a broken limb. Teach me how to move on without you in my life.*

I repeated this ritual for weeks, begging for insight. Every task I had to do, from picking my son up at school to cooking dinner, seemed monumental. I was unsure I'd ever feel peace again.

That was eighteen months ago. Today, my life is quite different. For one, I've become a football fan, which has surprised both my husband and me. Watching the New England Patriots win the Superbowl, I recalled fondly the many moments as a child that I watched sports with my father. I felt a tiny ache in my heart, sad that he couldn't share the excitement of the win with me.

Yet my dad is present in a new, richer way. The memories of him cheering on the Patriots and later calling my husband to discuss the football pool are a vivid part of me now. I feel such gratitude for the laughter and silliness we shared.

149

After spending so much time in the dark tunnel of grief, I want more of that lighter side of life. I am re-entering the world a transformed person.

Through my grief I have grown, through many, many baby steps. To move forward, I made choices, even if they were uncomfortable. These included going to the grocery store when it seemed easier to sit frozen in anxiety on the sofa, teaching a class when I felt safer to be alone than reaching out to others, and working on two books when I wasn't sure what to do with my sadness.

I am no longer "Daddy's little girl" who can cling to him and others for help and answers. While I miss the affection that role brought me, I know it was time for me to grow up.

I am my own woman, free to express myself in ways I had suppressed before. There are passages in this book, for example, I wouldn't dare write if my father were to view them. The way I relate to my mother and brother is also different than my father's order "to get along." Sometimes I need to challenge my mother to dress properly when I'm taking her out, and other times I need to back off from my brother's angry outbursts and not deal with him until he treats me respectfully.

I'm not living out my father's life anymore. While he supported me in many ways, he also once told me when I was begging to go to college, "Why would you want to do that? You're just going to get married and stay home with children someday." The possibility that I could also express myself through a career was never mentioned. He set limits, which I've worked hard to dismantle.

My daughter keeps telling me how proud she is that I am a writer, teacher, and personal and business coach, in addition to being a mother. She herself questions how she will be the special-needs teacher she wants to be and a mother, yet it's not an either-or dilemma she ponders. She is searching for ways to combine her gifts. I am modeling the possibility for her.

Lessons from Death

When we start at the center of ourselves we discover something worth-while extending toward the periphery of the circle. We find again some of the joy in the now, some of the peace in the here, some of the love in me and thee which go to make up the kingdom of heaven on earth.

—Anne Murrow Lindbergh, *Gift from the Sea*

One suggestion I offer to anyone in their forties is to be sure they have on hand a dark suit or dress. I've spent a lot of time in the past few years going to funerals. Midlife is often a time of learning about loss.

Yet at every funeral I've attended, the eulogies always focus on love and family. No one reads the résumé achievements. In the end, they don't seem to matter as much as what type of person the deceased was.

When I teach people to first discover who they are, not necessarily focus on what they do, I'm often met with much resistance. It's no different for the woman who says she is "just a mom" than it is for the CEO who defines herself by her external success.

Beneath those roles and titles is a person, born with a unique talent or gift to express to the world. Few people whom I have polled over the years have asked themselves this most central question: *What is my purpose/reason for living?*

It's a question that can take a long time to answer, but becomes much more meaningful once we recognize our own mortality.

A priest who has been at the bedside of thousands of patients told Oprah that the two most frequently asked questions by the dying person are:

**SURVIVING
TRAGEDIES**

What Does It Mean to
Say "Yes" to Life? To
Trust Life? (according to
Robert Veninnga, *A Gift
of Hope*)

• Living in the present,
taking one day at a
time.

• Pushing aside doubts
that you can ever again
be happy.

• Relying on friends,
asking them for com-
fort.

• Telling others how you
feel: lonely, fearful,
hopeful.

• Affirming that you are
good. Your intentions
are good. Your past
has been good. Your
future will be good.

• Meditating. Asking for
strength.

• When you affirm that
you can again trust life
your healing begins in
earnest.

1. Am I loved?
2. Did I love well?

The priest elaborated, noting that
the one thing death does not take away
from us is our ability to love.

I've left each funeral with a greater
desire to extend myself to others, to
express my wholeness to the world. It's
now or never, not when my kids go off to
college, the mortgage is paid, or some
other more convenient time.

EPILOGUE: THE THREE P'S

But most of our lives are governed by beliefs about possibility or success or happiness that we've picked up unconsciously over the years. The key is to take those beliefs and make sure they work for you, that they're effective and empowering.

—Anthony Robbins, *Unlimited Power*

Imagine if as a young child or adolescent you had no one to ask questions of and you never got any feedback. No one praised you or taught you of any of life's most basic skills, from how to do laundry to the appropriate way to greet an acquaintance. Hurts and fears were ignored because the incompetent adults surrounding you could not acknowledge your feelings. Worse, you were expected to care for the adults who were supposed to be protecting and guiding you.

There was no one to call for help, you thought, so you plowed your way through day by day, afraid to express any need. Life became survival, a boot camp of sorts.

Now, fast-forward to adulthood. What beliefs do you think such a child would carry forth into work and love relationships—the two areas, when properly balanced, can give us our greatest self-esteem?

I will tell you my experience as that young child and adult:

- The world is a lonely, frightening place.
- Life is extraordinarily hard.
- I am invisible to others; I don't matter.
- I need to help others before myself; their needs are more important.

153

• I am not safe; no one will help or protect me.
• I have to survive on my own; there is no sense of community, never has been, never will be.

These beliefs were my frame of reference for *most* of my adult life. I say *most* because I *slowly* learned to let go of beliefs that no longer served me and created new beliefs that are nourishing.

The beauty of transitions—however frightening, exciting, painful, or enlightening they may be--is that they give us an opportunity to heal our pasts and create new stories about our lives. We change the story by creating environments that support us to move forward and by unearthing and altering the beliefs that no longer serve us. Some experts believe it takes at least forty days of conscious effort to change a belief, but before we can change a belief we no longer want, we need to make it conscious.

A long time ago I came across this statistic: Only 13 percent of children who come from childhoods as dysfunctional as mine end up thriving in adulthood.

I did not become an expert on transition by default; I was determined and destined to change the deck of cards I was dealt. Even the quote I chose to place under my high school yearbook picture read, "Life is the continual remaking of yourself so at last you know how to live."

Many external events led me forward before I began consciously creating supportive beliefs. I became a reporter, an editor, a public relations executive, a wife, a mother, an entrepreneur, and eventually the writer, teacher, and personal life coach I am today. Each of these roles was a piece of a puzzle that led me to my purpose: to teach spiritual principles in a practical way and to help adults in transition connect with themselves and others encountering life change.

Had I not been a reporter and editor, I may not have learned to write. Had I not been a public relations executive, I may not have learned to market my workshops, my coaching practice, and my book. Had I not been a wife and mother, I may not have learned to seek a life of balance, combining work with family. I may have remained a workaholic. Had I not been an entrepreneur, I may not have created workshops from scratch that help adults in transition and then started another business as a personal life coach.

And had I not grown up feeling alone in a dysfunctional family, I may not have suffered the agony of isolation each time I made a major change in my life. Solitude is important for growth—isolation is not. Today, I love supporting people who are exploring new visions for themselves by coaching them one on one and helping them connect with other groups of nourishment. The support of a coach and/or group can help people stretch in ways they may not dare to do alone.

While the payoff for all my transitions is finding my authenticity and work and people I love, the search gave me many other insights. These are a few of them:

- Discover your childhood wounds and the part they play out in your life today. Initially, I unknowingly chose careers that were fast paced, chaotic, and full of negative cynical people, because they resembled my childhood environment. It wasn't until I allowed my nurturing nature to be expressed that I understood the unhappiness of my other careers.

  I married a man who is kind and passive, like my father was, which meant for me that once again I had to be the strong "go-getter," and even at times, a rescuer. It was painful to replay that role once again when a softer, more feminine side of me was aching to be released.

  Questions to ask yourself, both about love and work, are: Are you living out your childhood wounds? Are you honoring your parents' dreams instead of your own? Does your life reflect the highest vision you have for yourself?

- Trust your inner knowing no matter what the experts or media are telling you. I knew I had to sell my PR business, even though most people thought I was crazy to give up a lucrative lifestyle. I get more joy from writing eight hours for no pay than working one day in high tech for $1,500.

- Stepping off the fast track is scary, but once you're off you can't imagine ever living so disconnected to yourself and your loved ones again.

Most importantly, through the four major transitions detailed in this book, I've learned three words that at any moment can change the course of life and help you untap the beliefs that no longer serve you.

These words are: pause, pace, and participate. Knowing which of these words to act on requires trusting yourself and the inner whispers of guidance that come forth in the silence of solitude as well from the conversations of friends and even strangers.

Pause

How many times have you made a mistake because you hurried into something? I knew before even starting my public relations business with a friend that the partnership was off-balance. I pushed forward anyway, determined to make the business succeed, despite the friction. Years later, another woman who also suffered the pain of dismantling a business started with a friend said, "My lawyer is right. Partners are for dancing."

Sometimes, instead of pausing for the answers to come, we "will" a direction. We make the new job or the new boyfriend appear better than they are so we can move forward. What we may have needed to do instead was simply stop and be uncomfortable where we are for a while.

Other times, if we're risking new ways of being, like when we fall in love, we need to pause while the unfamiliar is settling in. When I have met new people who are emotionally present and acknowledge me, I have had to pause to let in the feedback and support I was not accustomed to accepting.

Pace

After pausing, we eventually need to move forward if we are to grow. In younger days I rushed forward, eager to embrace a new challenge, stampeding any feelings of fear I may have had, staying so busy I couldn't feel anything.

Through my many transitions, I've learned to accept my feelings as my friends. I don't want to push them aside anymore; they guide me. In order to feel them, I need to pace myself and listen. I've wanted to publish this book for a long time, but I also wanted to live the life of balance that I teach. I chose to write part-time while raising my young children. I didn't want to spend hours marketing the book until my children were both in school full-time. I felt ready to bring the book forth after working on it for twelve years. That longer time span gave the book more depth and diversity. I was able to write and teach about four transitions instead of one, as I had originally planned.

Participate

What one word can change someone from a couch potato to a fitness addict, from a bored housewife to a clever part-time professional, from an unhappy spouse to a loving marriage partner, from an aspiring writer to a published author, from a laid-off executive to a creative entrepreneur, from a distant acquaintance to a caring friend?

"Participate" is the word.

Not just participate, but participate fully. Set the intention that you will act to the best of your ability.

I remember when I was starting my first business. I was twenty-eight years old, single, and had hardly any savings. A few weeks before I quit my job to start the business, my Toyota Corolla was stolen from the parking lot of the apartment building in which I was living. I needed to replace the car. I was unsure whether to purchase another Corolla or the more expensive Toyota Camry.

"Get the Camry," my dad said. "That way you will be sure your business will succeed."

Getting the Camry did make me reach higher and engage my full self in the business. It made me participate, not cruise along and wait for something to happen.

Focusing on the word "participate" has helped me move beyond many fears. You either choose to participate or stay in the fear. You can't do both.

When inertia returns and I don't feel like playing with my children, cooking dinner, making love, meeting a friend, exercising, or even writing, I remind myself: participate. I usually end up feeling better when I choose to act instead of observe.

I end this book, excited about being a published author, even though I am quite scared about sharing intimate details of my soul's unfolding with the masses. I take the risk of using my life as an example, knowing I am being called to help others understand more fully the emotional upheaval of transition.

I will continue to collaborate with clients who are committed to personal growth and development, feeling honored to witness another human being's evolution. I know that if I can beat the odds of a highly dysfunctional beginning to life that any person who walks into my office can reach his or her highest potential too. We all have the power to change our thoughts, no matter what our background.

Most importantly, I know I am blessed.

Twelve years ago I asked an early mentor of mine what happens after we dig through the pain and excavate false beliefs. "You feel lighter," she responded. Back then, her simple answer didn't seem quite convincing.

Now, after my excavation into the depths of my soul through the transitions detailed in this book, I understand what "feeling lighter" means. My days are brighter, but not painless. I don't feel as much fear or have the need to control things. Instead, a challenge is "here comes another lesson." We can learn as much from love, laughter, and fun as through adversity.

I have felt magic in what I call "marshmallow moments," times during the day when I know I am touched by God's grace. I feel like I'm floating or am spongy like a marshmallow. Pure joy. A feeling of being lifted. Relief. Contentment.

These moments happen when I understand something I didn't comprehend before, when I'm truly present to another, or when I feel compassion for or touch another's soul. I feel these moments when I'm sitting attentively with my daughter, Catie, at a local café and she simply smiles at me; reading a book with my son, Brendan, cuddled in bed; walking hand in hand with Catie to the local bird sanctuary; writing in my office sanctuary and watching five deer prance by; talking with my brother, knowing that he and I shared a great adventure that once tore us apart and now bonds us together; walking the beach and seeing a passerby look into my eyes with kindness, understanding, and acceptance; voicing anger or discontent and having someone listen with concern instead of withdraw in fright; watching a truck video or humbly trying to build Lego blocks with my son, the construction expert; seeing firsthand how vastly unique men and women are and learning to appreciate the differences; rejoicing in a client's breakthrough or watching a student connect with another in integrity or vulnerability; and when I feel from the depths of my soul that my life and work have purpose and meaning.

Yes, my life with all its challenges is a gift, and so is yours. Cherish the journey, even when it takes unexpected turns.

Gail Kauranen Jones's Biography

Gail Kauranen Jones lives a passionate life writing books, teaching workshops about transition, and working as a personal and business coach.

She is a member of the International Women's Writing Guild, the International Coach Federation (ICF), Business Network International (BNI), and Coachville's Graduate School of Coaching and Small Business School of Coaching.

For more information about her work, view her Web site: www.SupportMatters.com.

Printed in the United States
75899LV00003B/105